AMERICAN POLITICAL, ECONOMIC, AND SECURITY ISSUES

SAVINGS SHIFTS IN AMERICA

TRENDS AND POLICIES

AMERICAN POLITICAL, ECONOMIC, AND SECURITY ISSUES

Additional books in this series can be found on Nova's website under the Series tab.

Additional E-books in this series can be found on Nova's website under the E-books tab.

ECONOMIC ISSUES, PROBLEMS AND PERSPECTIVES

Additional books in this series can be found on Nova's website under the Series tab.

Additional E-books in this series can be found on Nova's website under the E-books tab.

AMERICAN POLITICAL, ECONOMIC, AND SECURITY ISSUES

SAVINGS SHIFTS IN AMERICA

TRENDS AND POLICIES

CONSTANTINA AZZARÀ
EDITOR

Nova Science Publishers, Inc.
New York

Library of Congress Cataloging-in-Publication Data

Savings shifts in America : trends and policies / editor, Constantina Azzar`.
p. cm.
Includes index.
ISBN 978-1-61470-392-1 (softcover)
1. Saving and investment--United States. 2. Consumer credit--United States. 3. Debt--United States. I. Azzar`, Constantina.
HC110.S3S283 2011
339.4'30973--dc23

2011024324

Published by Nova Science Publishers, Inc. † New York

CONTENTS

PREFACE

The amount of money saved has important consequences. Nationally, the amount of saving affects how much can be invested and ultimately the size of the capital stock. Increasing the size of the capital stock is believed to be one way to raise the productivity of the labor force and the economy's long-term growth rate. Individually, saving is critical to accumulating sufficient wealth to maintain living standards after retirement. The pace of economic growth is likely to be a matter of particular importance in the decades just ahead as the economy confronts the need to effect unprecedented generational transfer of income to pay for the retirement of the baby-boom generation. This book examines how national saving is measured, presents recent estimates of saving rates in the U.S. and provides those of other major industrial countries.

Chapter 1- Household balance sheets have been a subject of recurrent legislative interest. Over the past decades, Congress has enacted consumer bankruptcy reform; legislation to guide credit card lending and predatory lending; a range of mortgage modification programs; tax provisions to encourage saving or change the cost of borrowing; initiatives to expand mortgage lending to low- and middle-income families; and has established a new federal agency to monitor consumer finance. Such activity has taken place against a backdrop of over four decades of steadily rising household debt.

Chapter 4- The amount of money saved has important economic consequences. Nationally, the amount of saving affects how much can be invested and ultimately the size of the capital stock. Increasing the size of the capital stock is believed to be one way to raise the productivity of the labor force and the economy's long-term growth rate. Individually, saving is critical to accumulating sufficient wealth to maintain living standards after retirement. This report explains how national saving is measured, presents recent estimates of saving rates in the United States, and, for comparison, provides those of other major industrial countries.

Chapter 3- Household saving matters for two reasons. First, it is an important source of funds to finance domestic investment. Second, it is the means by which workers accumulate wealth and maintain their living standard into retirement. Congress has indicated its desire to promote household saving by, among other things, creating individual retirement accounts, and saving is an important consideration in proposals to reform Social Security. At a time, however, when policymakers have been looking for ways to increase spending to minimize the downturn and get the economy growing again, households have begun to save more.

Chapter 4- Saving is the portion of national output that is not consumed and represents resources that can be used to increase, replace, or improve the nation's capital stock. The U.S. net national saving rate reached a post-war peak of 12.4% in 1965 and has then trended downward since to a low of -0.2% in 2008. Many analysts claim that saving is too low. Among the Organization for Economic Cooperation and Development (OECD) countries, the United States has the fourth lowest saving rate.

In: Savings Shifts in America
Editor: Constantina Azzarà
ISBN: 978-1-61470-392-1

Chapter 1

HOUSEHOLD DELEVERAGING: WHY IS CONSUMER DEBT FALLING?*

Mark Jickling and Darryl E. Getter

SUMMARY

Household balance sheets have been a subject of recurrent legislative interest. Over the past decades, Congress has enacted consumer bankruptcy reform; legislation to guide credit card lending and predatory lending; a range of mortgage modification programs; tax provisions to encourage saving or change the cost of borrowing; initiatives to expand mortgage lending to low- and middle-income families; and has established a new federal agency to monitor consumer finance. Such activity has taken place against a backdrop of over four decades of steadily rising household debt.

In the third quarter of 2008, the amount of debt held by U.S. households began to fall and has continued to decline for 10 consecutive quarters. In all, households have reduced their debt burden by about $707 billion, or 5.4%. This trend is unprecedented in postwar U.S. history. The process of debt reduction, or deleveraging, by American consumers has important implications for the economy. Debt is generally used to finance consumption, which accounts for about 70% of gross domestic product. Falling debt implies slower consumption growth, which in turn slows

* This is an edited, reformatted and augmented version of a Congressional Research Service publication, CRS Report for Congress R41623, from www.crs.gov, dated March 11, 2011.

business investment. Thus, continued household deleveraging may become a drag on the economic recovery and limit the effectiveness of legislative efforts to create jobs.

The ultimate impact of deleveraging depends on uncertain factors: (1) how long the current trend continues, (2) how far household debt balances fall, and (3) whether deleveraging represents a lasting change in consumer behavior or simply a reflection of the recession and financial crisis that began in 2007, which caused significant losses in wealth to consumers and serious distress to lenders.

Debt balances are determined by three trends: (1) new borrowing by households, (2) repayment of existing debts, and (3) charge-offs, or writedowns, of debt that lenders believe is uncollectible. All three appear to play some part in recent deleveraging. Charge-off rates for mortgage debt and other forms of consumer credit rose well above historical norms after 2007 (though they began to decline in 2010). Consumers have accelerated repayment of certain debts, including mortgages, where many refinancing transactions now involve payment of principal to reduce the debt outstanding. Household borrowing appears to have fallen, yet it is difficult to disentangle supply and demand effects. Are consumers voluntarily reducing use of credit to improve their finances or are lenders more stringent about making new loans? The answer appears to be both, based on the limited evidence available.

Why would consumers change their attitude toward debt, after many decades of increased borrowing? One plausible explanation involves losses to household wealth from falling stock and home prices. Loss of wealth, particularly in real estate, may trigger defaults on debt and may spur households to seek to restore precautionary wealth balances by increasing their saving. The loss of stock market wealth in 2000 did not lead to deleveraging. What is different since 2008 is the drop in the price of houses, assets on which many households still owe money. The last time a significant drop in house prices occurred was during the Great Depression, which was also the last time sustained household deleveraging happened in the United States.

This report presents information that documents household deleveraging and discusses several possible demand and supply explanations.

INTRODUCTION

Over the past 40 years, household debt has generally risen, regardless of macroeconomic or financial conditions. Even during recessions prior to 2007, household borrowing increased. In the most recent 2007-2009 recession, however, household debt began to decline. The fall in household debt balances began in the third quarter of 2008 and has continued for 10 consecutive quarters through the last quarter of 2010 (the latest period for which data are available).

Household deleveraging, or debt reduction, may have important implications for the economy. Continued deleveraging could be a drag on an economic recovery that already appears weak, especially in job creation.[1] As households curtail consumption, which typically accounts for approximately 70% of gross domestic product (GDP), in order to reduce their debt or rebuild nest eggs for retirement, education, and other purposes, the dampening effect on economic recovery could be significant.[2] Damaged household balance sheets following asset price declines may be translating into defaults that weaken lender balance sheets, prompting lenders to restrict the supply of credit. Fiscal policy initiatives, such as tax cuts and spending increases, designed to stimulate the economy may not be as effective as in previous recessions given that households and lender balance sheets have been significantly affected.[3]

This report presents data illustrating household deleveraging since 2008 and contrasts this episode to previous trends in household credit use. It also presents various explanations for deleveraging. One possibility is that after a long period during which debt grew at a faster rate than income, changes in preferences of households may have reduced the demand for credit. Another factor that may be reducing demand for credit is the loss of wealth that occurs as house prices fall. Given that household net worth—assets minus liabilities—fell sharply during the 2007-2009 recession, the demand for credit may have declined because households had fewer financial resources with which to secure and repay loans. A decline in wealth may have triggered household defaults on existing debt obligations, forcing lenders to write off more uncollectible loans.

Lenders who were highly leveraged going into the financial crisis have since sought to reduce certain types of risky liabilities, leading to a contraction in the supply of credit. Both households and financial institutions are seeking to strengthen their balance sheets, meaning that both supply and demand factors may be contributing to household deleveraging, and slowing the pace of economic recovery.

An Appendix to this report presents information on household deleveraging during the Great Depression.

RECENT HOUSEHOLD DELEVERAGING PATTERNS

Figure 1 shows the level of household debt outstanding since 1968 in three categories: home mortgages, revolving or credit card debt, and nonrevolving credit, which consists primarily of automobile and student loan debt.[4]

Figure 1 indicates that household debt consists predominantly of mortgage debt. Falling home prices and a rise in defaults and foreclosures since 2007 account for a fall in mortgage balances outstanding. In addition, a significant share of the fall in mortgage debt outstanding can be attributed to home equity loans, which often substitute for other types of consumer credit.

Deleveraging has not been confined to mortgages. Revolving or credit card debt has also declined, falling by about 17.5% between the second quarter of 2008 and the fourth quarter of 2010. Nonrevolving credit has not shown much growth or decline since 2008, but the previous upward trend has been interrupted.

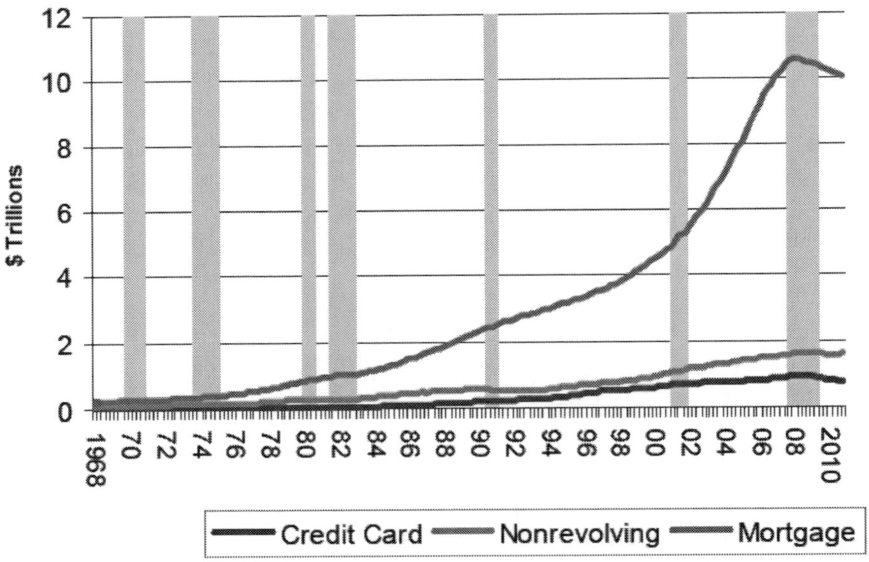

Source: Federal Reserve, *Flow of Funds Accounts* (Release Z.1) and *Consumer Credit* (Release G. 19).
Note: The grey bars indicate recessions.

Figure 1. Household Debt Outstanding, 1968-2010.

Table 1 and Figure 2 break down the decrease in household debt from the second quarter of 2008 through the fourth quarter of 2010, by type of loan.

Declines in home equity loans outstanding and credit card debt accounted for 49% of the fall in household debt through the fourth quarter of 2010, about equal to the drop in other (non-home equity) mortgage debt.

Table 1. Summary of Changes in Household Debt, 2008-2010

	Debt Outstanding (in billions of dollars)		Change from 2nd Qtr 2008 through 3rd Qtr 2010	
Type of Debt	2nd Qtr, 2008	4th Qtr, 2010	($ Billions)	(Percentage)
Home Mortgage	10,608	10,125	-538	-5.1
Home Equity Loans	1,127	975	-179	-15.8
Revolving Credit	970	806	-170	-17.5
Nonrevolving Credit	1,606	1,590	-1	-0.1
Total	13,184	12,521	-707	-5.4

Source: Federal Reserve, *Flow of Funds Accounts* (Release Z.1) and *Consumer Credit* (Release G. 19).

Note: Home equity loans are a subset of home mortgage debt.

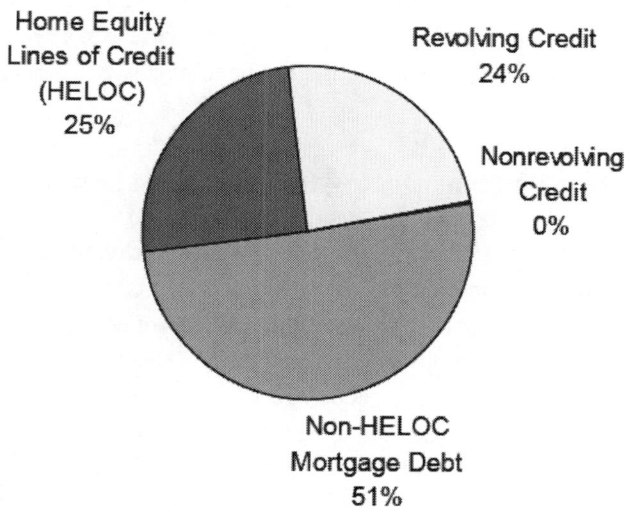

Source: Federal Reserve, *Flow of Funds Accounts* (Release Z.1) and *Consumer Credit* (Release G. 19).

Figure 2. Shares in the Decline of Household Debt Outstanding, by Type of Credit, Second Quarter 2008 through Fourth Quarter 2010, (Percentage of Total Decline of $707 Billion).

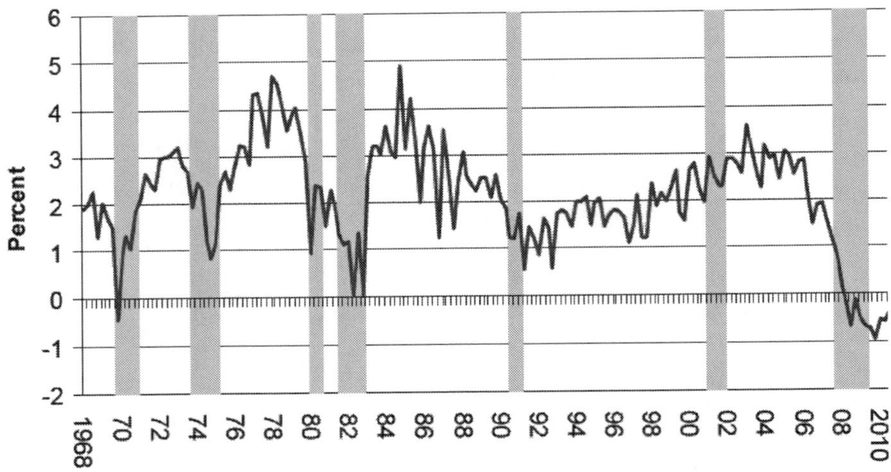

Source: Federal Reserve, *Flow of Funds Accounts* (Release Z.1) and *Consumer Credit* (Release G. 19). Note: The grey bars indicate recessions.

Figure 3. Quarterly Percent Change in Total Household Debt Outstanding, 1968-2010.

Figure 3 illustrates the quarterly percentage change in total household debt balances since 1968. Total household debt balances increased during every quarter between 1968 and 2008, except for one quarter in 1970. Since the second quarter of 2008, the rate of change has been negative.

Household Debt Patterns During Recent Recessions

Figure 3 suggests that the growth rate in household debt tends to fall in and around periods of economic recession. To address the question of whether post-2008 deleveraging is simply a normal cyclical phenomenon, Figure 4, Figure 5, and Figure 6 compare changes in household credit outstanding during and after the four most recent recessions.[5] For each category of household debt, an index has been constructed in which amounts of debt outstanding have been normalized to the first month or quarter of the recession.[6] The indices allow percentage changes in aggregate debt movements to be compared. Figure 4 reflects changes in home mortgage debt outstanding; Figure 5 shows changes in credit card debt outstanding; and Figure 6 shows the index that reflects changes in nonrevolving credit outstanding.

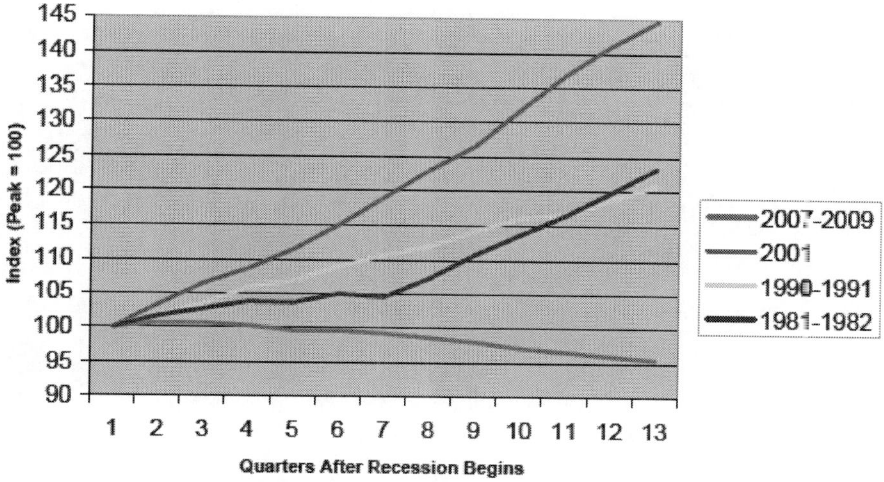

Source: Federal Reserve, *Flow of Funds Accounts* (Release Z.1).
Note: Index calculations by CRS.

Figure 4. Mortgage Debt in Recessions, 1981-2009.

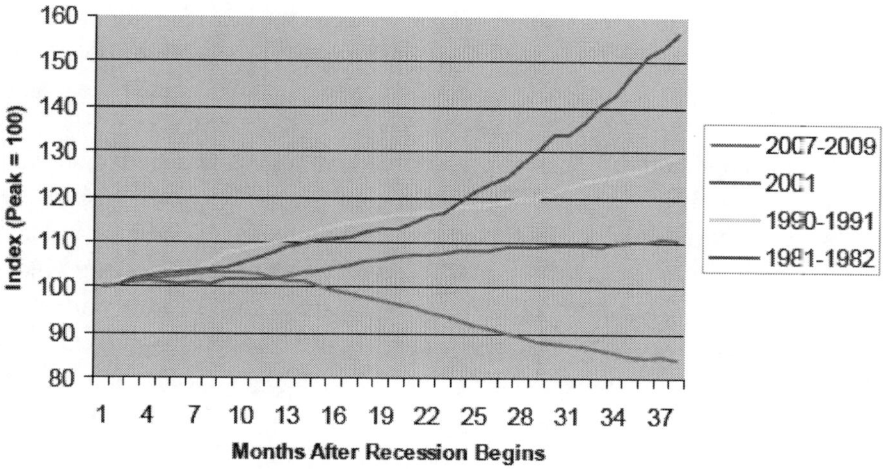

Source: : Federal Reserve, *Consumer Credit* (Release G. 19).
Note: Index calculations by CRS.

Figure 5. Credit Card Debt in Recessions, 1981-2009.

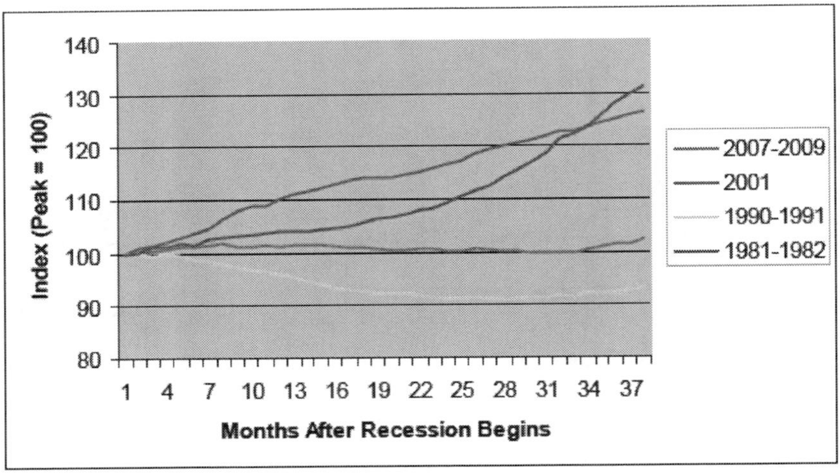

Source: Federal Reserve, *Consumer Credit* (Release G. 19).
Note: Index calculations by CRS.

Figure 6. Nonrevolving Debt in Recessions, 1981-2009.

The figures show trends in debt for 13 quarters or 38 months[7] after each cyclical peak, which is the amount of time between the beginning of the 2007-2009 recession and the latest period for which data are available. Hence, the indices cover the recessions and extend into the subsequent economic recoveries.

Figure 4 and Figure 5 show that a decline in mortgage and credit card debt balances was unique to the 2007-2009 recession. The amount of mortgage and credit card debt outstanding continued to grow in the other recessions and into the economic recoveries that followed. The behavior of nonrevolving credit, shown in Figure 6, was different. Nonrevolving credit rose steadily during the 1981-1982 and 2001 recessions; has been relatively flat since the beginning of the 2007-2009 recession; but declined during the 1990-1991 recession by over 7%.[8] Even allowing for the behavior of nonrevolving debt, however, the indices show that deleveraging has not been a common feature in economic contractions during the past 30 years.

CAUSES OF DELEVERAGING

An analysis of factors that can influence trends in household debt may be useful to understand why households are deleveraging and the policy implications of recent trends. Changes in debt balances are determined by three flows:

- new borrowing by households,
- repayment of existing debt, and
- charge-offs (or writedowns) of debt that lenders believe is uncollectible.

New borrowing is affected by either supply or demand factors—lenders may restrict the supply of new credit or consumers may become less inclined to borrow. Similarly, consumers may voluntarily accelerate debt repayment, and lenders may call in existing debts (although their ability to do so is limited under most consumer debt contracts). Loan charge-offs do not fit neatly into either the supply or the demand category. Charge-offs reduce the level of debt outstanding, and thus may be viewed as a reduction in the supply of debt. On the other hand, in some cases, borrowers exercise control over when and whether to default on a loan, so an increase in chargeoffs may also reflect consumers desire to reduce their debt levels.

The sections that follow consider various explanations for deleveraging that are based on (1) a drop in consumer demand, (2) lender restrictions on the supply of credit, and (3) the extent to which rising loan charge-off rates account for the drop in debt levels, even in the absence of any change in lender or borrower behavior.

Demand-Side Explanations

Household demand for credit may have declined for any of the following reasons:

- after a steady, decades-long rise, household debt may have finally reached unsustainable levels;
- a decline in household net worth, which occurred as a result of falling asset values during the recession of 2007-2009, may have induced households to rebuild their savings balances as precautionary measures; or
- the decline in household net worth may have increased the incidence of default.

Unsustainable Household Debt Levels

Access to credit has allowed many families to better their lot, but the expansion of consumer lending over the past decades has also caused concerns. As debt rose, so did bankruptcy rates[9] and financial distress.[10] Some households may have used debt to avoid constraints on consumption imposed by their incomes.[11] Since 1968, growth in household debt has outpaced growth in disposable income—a trend that could not be sustained indefinitely. At some point, it could be argued that the trend had to reverse itself. This explanation will be referred to as the unsustainable debt hypothesis.[12]

A problem with this hypothesis that there is no analytical method for determining the point at which debt becomes "unsustainable." Some commentators look at the ratio of total debt outstanding to disposable personal income, which is presented in Figure 7.[13] This ratio may be difficult to interpret given that disposable personal income represents a flow measure (one year of earnings), while debt outstanding represents a stock measure (debt which is expected to be repaid over a longer time horizon). Although ultimately debt repayment must come out of household income, it does not have to do so in a single year. Hence, this measure may be a misleading indicator of unsustainable leverage.

Nonetheless, the debt-to-income ratio shows that households have taken on debt faster than their incomes have grown. There must be a limit to debt growth if incomes do not keep pace, even if the limit cannot be determined in advance.

From an individual household's point of view, the total amount of debt it carries is generally less important than the proportion of its resources that it must devote to debt service. The Federal Reserve calculates a ratio that compares current income and debt payments. This debt service ratio, expressed as the percentage of income that goes to repay debt, reflects three variables: income, the amount of debt, and the cost of debt, or the interest rate. Figure 8 tracks changes in the debt service ratio between 1980 and the third quarter of 2010.

The debt service ratio fluctuates between 11% and 12% between 1980 and 2000, climbs to about 14% in 2005, and then falls back into the earlier range after deleveraging begins in 2008. At least two interpretations of these data are possible. One may observe the rise from 2000 through 2007 and argue that 14 cents of each dollar earned represented an unsustainable debt burden, and so debt had to fall. On the other hand, the rise in the debt burden was not as steep as the rise in debt or the debt-to-income ratio. Households have been able to borrow more without a corresponding increase in the debt burden because of the decline in interest rates since 1980.

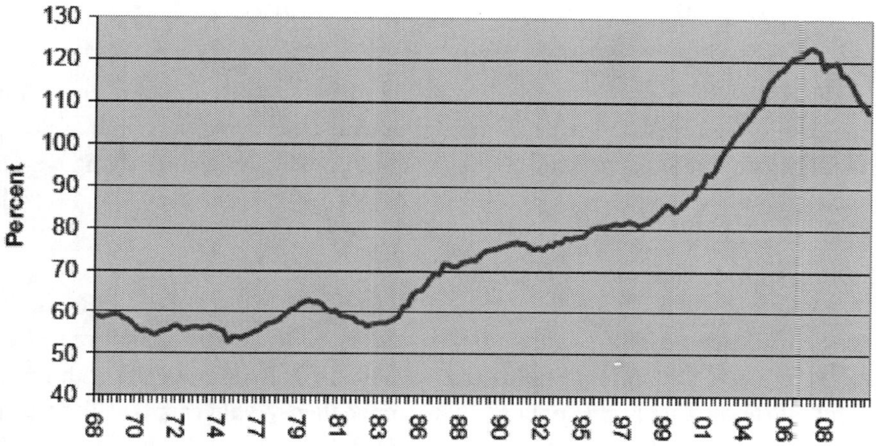

Source: Federal Reserve and Bureau of Economic Analysis.

Figure 7. Household Debt Outstanding as a Percentage of Disposable Personal Income, 1968-2010.

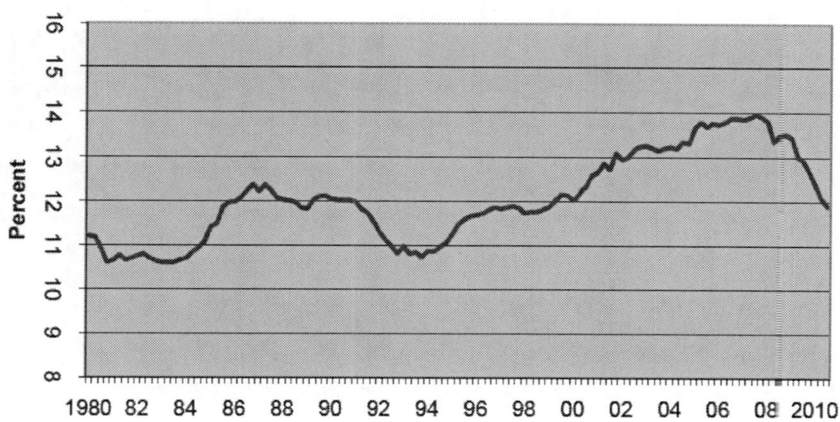

Source: Federal Reserve, Household Debt Service and Financial Obligations Ratios.

Figure 8. Debt Service Ratio, 1980-2010.

The increase in the debt burden since 1980 has been much less extreme than the increase in debt outstanding, which was about six times higher at the 2007 peak than in 1980. This difference creates difficulties for the hypothesis in that the dramatic rise in the debt-to-income ratio indicates that debt had reached an unsustainable level. Because the rise in the cost of debt service was relatively moderate compared with the increase in debt outstanding, is rising debt-to-income enough to explain a significant shift in household financial behavior?

In effect, the hypothesis that debt began to fall because it had risen for too long and to excessive levels is an argument that there was a bubble in household debt that had to end. It does not help establish the underlying causes of such a bubble.

Contraction in Household Wealth

Other explanations for deleveraging focus on the effects of a decline in the value of household real estate and financial assets. The 2007-2009 recession was a period in which households lost trillions of dollars in wealth as a result of falling home and stock prices.[14] Economic theory suggests that a drop in household net worth—assets minus liabilities—may cause households to reduce borrowing and spending as they attempt to repair their balance sheets, and that it may also trigger a rise in the incidence of default.

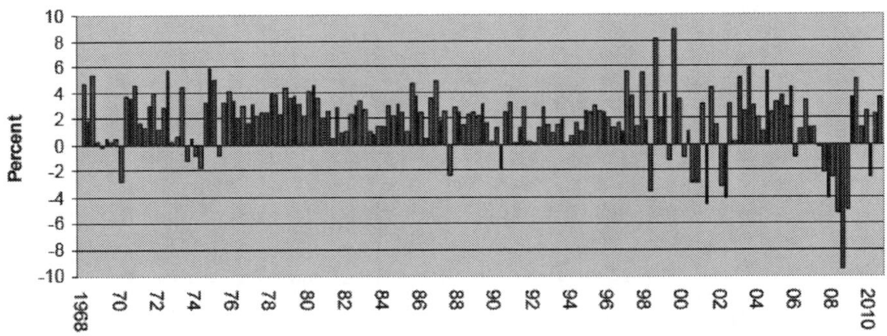

Source: Federal Reserve, *Flow of Funds Accounts*, Table B.100.
Note: These figures include the non-profit sector.

Figure 9. Quarterly Changes in Household Net Worth, 1968-2010.

Figure 9 shows estimated changes in quarterly household net worth since 1968. (Household net worth is defined as the difference between the value of household assets and liabilities.) Net worth fell for seven consecutive quarters beginning in mid-2007, which appears to be without precedent in the 1968-2010 period. Several quarterly drops were also recorded during the 2000-2002 period, which coincided with the "dot.com" stock market crash, but household deleveraging did not take place then, as the charts above that compare recent recessions indicate.

Figure 10 illustrates changes in household net worth for 13 quarters after the start of the four most recent recessions. An index has been constructed in which the percentage changes in household net worth over the three-year period are normalized to the first quarter of the recession. Figure 10 suggests that households experienced a much larger reduction in their net worth during the 2007-2009 recession as compared with previous recessions.

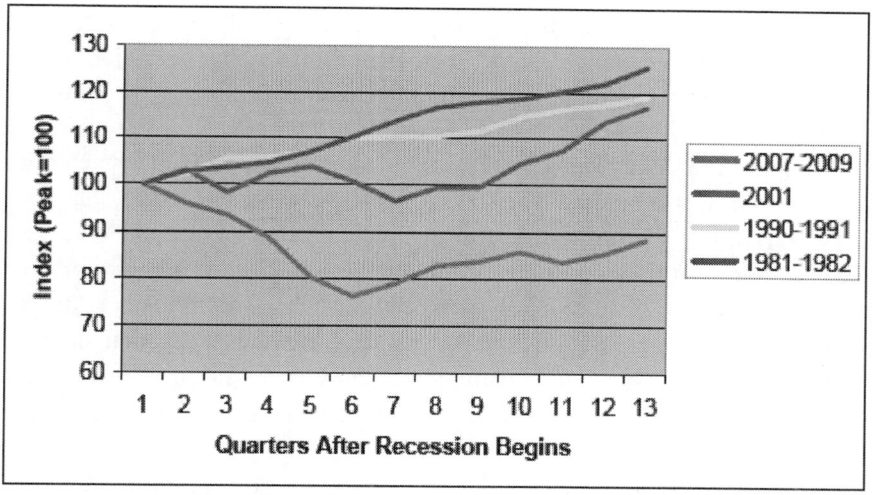

Source: Federal Reserve, *Flow of Funds Accounts*, Table B.100.
Note: These figures include the non-profit sector.

Figure 10. Household Net Worth in Recessions, 1981-2009.

Economic theory suggests two mechanisms by which a fall in household asset values may lead to a decline in the demand for credit. These are discussed below.

Deleveraging for Precautionary Reasons

Households may have a precautionary savings motive that leads them to reduce borrowing when household wealth drops. If households wish to maintain a certain balance of wealth to protect themselves against unexpected economic reversals, their behavior will change when that balance is eroded. Households may reduce spending and increase saving until their precautionary store of wealth has been replenished to more comfortable levels.[15] In other words, borrowing at previous levels may be less desirable after net worth declines, and some households may choose to borrow less in order to improve their financial situations. This is the first channel, or mechanism, by which a fall in net worth might have triggered a change in household debt levels. The second relates to default.

Deleveraging by Defaulting on Loans

Economic theory relates default behavior to "trigger events" or sudden changes in life circumstances, such as job loss, divorce, or illness; a sudden loss in net worth may also constitute such a trigger event.[16] Federal Reserve data indicates that default rates in all three categories of household debt rose sharply after 2007, leading to higher loan charge-offs by banks, which directly reduce the amount of debt outstanding. (These data appear in Figure 12 below.)

Why would falling asset values raise the incidence of default? Much of the decline in net worth since 2007 is attributable to real estate assets that many households financed through borrowing and on which they still owe debt. According to CoreLogic, in the third quarter of 2010, 10.8 million U.S. mortgages (22.5% of the total) were underwater, which means that the homeowner owed more than the market value of the house.[17] In that situation, the homeowner may have an incentive to default on the mortgage, and recent foreclosure statistics suggest that many homeowners have been responding to that incentive.[18]

While households also experienced significant losses during the stock market downturn associated with the financial crisis and recession, these losses may have had less impact on the incentive to default. Most households purchase stocks with cash—when prices fall, they suffer a loss in paper wealth, but they do not carry debt obligations based on the old, higher values. Investors commonly expect volatility in stock prices, which may lead them to believe that a sharp drop in value will be short-term (at least in comparison to real estate prices).[19] The distinction between the two types of assets may explain why multi-trillion-dollar stock losses during the "dot.com" crash in 2000-2002 and the 2001 recession did not trigger deleveraging.[20]

Supply-Side Explanations: Lender Retrenchment

The previous explanations involved factors influencing the demand for credit, but a reduction in the supply of credit may also matter. The financial crisis that began in 2007 exposed serious weaknesses in many financial institutions, and many lenders have since struggled to rebuild their capital positions. One way to meet or reduce regulatory capital requirements is to curtail the amount of risky loans on the books. Rising loan losses may encourage lenders to become more skeptical about extending new credit without greater assurances of repayment. Lenders may tighten underwriting standards and otherwise restrict the availability of new credit, especially for households judged more likely to default. Lenders may also reduce existing unused lines of credit in order to avoid an unwanted expansion of consumer loans.

The Federal Reserve's Senior Loan Officer Opinion Survey on Bank Lending Practices, which is conducted quarterly, asks bankers about changes in the standards and terms of bank lending as well as changes in the demand for loans.[21] Bankers are asked whether they expect to tighten or loosen the terms and conditions of various types of loans, and this provides insight into whether the supply of credit will expand or contract in the near future. The survey is less valuable as a long-term measure, because the responses compare present conditions to the immediately preceding period rather than over longer periods.[22] Nevertheless, the survey did show sharp increases in the number of banks tightening standards for credit card, mortgage, and other consumer loans beginning in 2007. The survey also indicated weaker consumer demand for loans during that period.

Figure 11 shows the results of the quarterly loan officer surveys conducted between 1996 and November 2010. The solid lines show the net percentage of loan officers who expect to tighten standards for credit card and other consumer loans. Positive values indicate a tightening credit supply while negative values mean that more banks are loosening standards than are tightening them. The dotted line shows responses to the question about whether demand for consumer loans is growing or shrinking. Negative values here indicate a perceived reduction in the demand for credit.

The data in Figure 11 show that loan standards tightened beginning in 2007, and that demand weakened more or less simultaneously. The data do not seem to provide evidence that these trends were a principal cause of deleveraging—a significant tightening of supply was observed in 1996 and 1997, and yet debt outstanding remained on an expansionary path, as Figure 3 shows. Perceived demand for credit plunged during 2000 and 2001, yet there was no deleveraging then, either.

Thus, while there is evidence that supply of credit tightened in 2007, as would be expected after the financial turmoil that began in that year, the surveys indicate that demand dropped as well. Data from the loan survey do not appear to answer the question of the relative importance of supply and demand factors in recent deleveraging. Moreover, it is not clear that the magnitude of these post-2007 supply and demand shifts were historically unprecedented, or that they explain the reversal in the long rise of household debt.

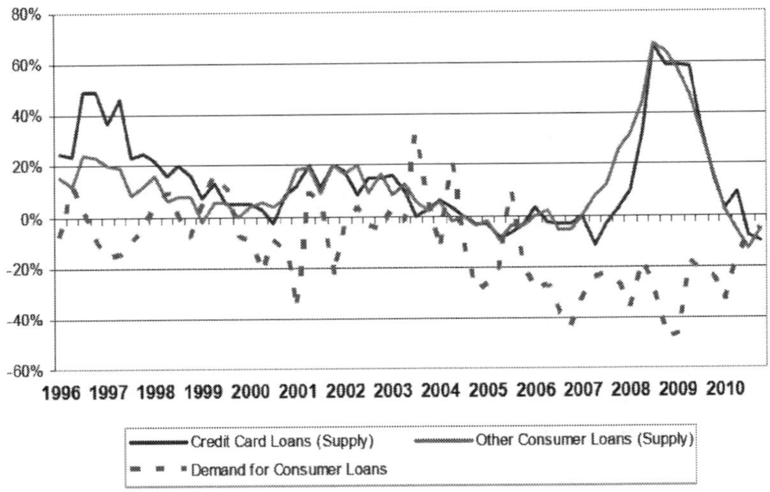

Source: Federal Reserve, Senior Loan Officer Opinion Survey on Bank Lending Practices.

Figure 11. Net Percentage of Banks Tightening or Loosening Consumer Credit Standards, and Demand for Consumer Loans: 1996-2010.

CAN THE EFFECTS OF DEMAND, SUPPLY, AND CHARGE-OFFS BE DISENTANGLED?

The report now takes a closer look at some of the evidence on deleveraging in particular loan markets to see how much can be explained by decreases in credit demand or supply or increases in the volume of loans charged-off. The basic Federal Reserve data on debt outstanding do not distinguish between slowdowns in new borrowing, contractions of lending, or charged-off debt. Other data bearing on credit card and mortgage lending, however, do shed partial light on the question.

Rising Loan Losses

Figure 12 shows charge-off rates for commercial bank loans in three categories: single-family residential mortgages, credit card debt, and other consumer loans. Charge-offs occur when lenders conclude that a debt will not be repaid, remove it from the books, and charge it against loss reserves. During the past few years, all three major categories of household debt experienced loss rates well above the historical norm.

Declining home prices and the phenomenon of underwater mortgages, as well as the loosening of mortgage underwriting standards during the boom (when many borrowers received loans that traditional underwriting standards would have deemed too large for their incomes), explain why mortgage charge-offs increased. There may have been some spillover from mortgages to other forms of debt, as households struggling to meet mortgage payments defaulted on credit card, automobile, or other loans to avoid foreclosure. This is consistent with the hypothesis discussed above of loss of wealth as a "trigger event" that may increase the propensity to default. (See "Deleveraging by Defaulting on Loans" section.)

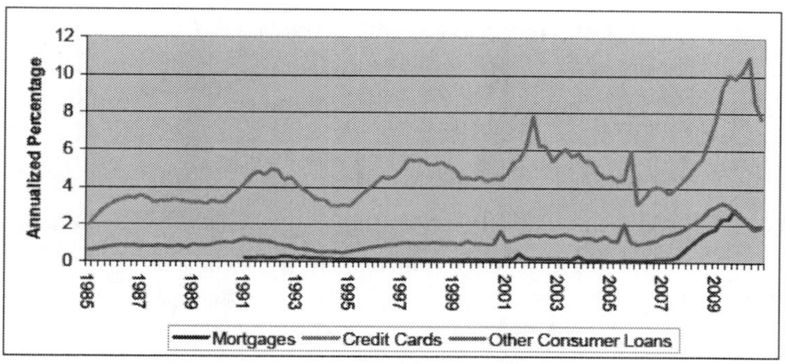

Source: Federal Reserve, Charge-Off and Delinquency Rates on Loans and Leases at Commercial Banks.

Notes: Single-family residential mortgage data available only from 1991.

Figure 12. Charge-Off Rates for Commercial Bank Loans to Households, 1985-2010 (Quarterly data at annual rates).

Some analysts have argued that charged-off loans account for nearly all of the observed deleveraging since 2008, implying that there has been little if any change in either consumer demand for or lender supply of credit.[23] The next section examines the degree to which recent deleveraging may be attributed to households defaulting on existing credit, as opposed to changes in the rates of new borrowing or lending.

Credit Card Deleveraging

Table 2 below presents estimates of the dollar amount of credit card debt charged off in each quarter since the beginning of 2005, and compares that to the actual reductions reported in the debt outstanding statistics. The second and third columns of Table 2 include the credit card charge-off rate data from Figure 12 and the credit card debt outstanding figures from Figure 1, from the first quarter of 2005 through the fourth quarter of 2010. The fourth column, which is calculated from columns two and three, presents dollar estimates of loans written off.[24] The amount of credit card debt charged off in recent years has increased substantially, as is implied by rising charge-off rates.

The fifth column in Table 2 shows the actual change in credit card debt outstanding from the previous quarter.[25] The difference between the actual change in credit card balances and the estimated value of loans charged-off must equal the net of the other two flows that determine the level of debt outstanding: new borrowing and repayment of existing debt. The sum of net new borrowing plus charge-offs equals the actual change in debt balances. This figure appears in the right-hand column as "Implied Net New Borrowing."[26]

The data in Table 2 show that while the value of credit card debt charged-off in recent years has increased substantially, there has also been a sharp drop in net new borrowing since 2008. Net new borrowing averaged $21.3 billion per quarter between the first quarter of 2005 and the third quarter of 2008; since then, it has averaged $57 million per quarter. Consumers must either be taking on less new debt, accelerating repayment of existing debt, or both. The figures in Table 2 do not indicate which it is.

A recent Federal Reserve Bank of New York study looks at changes in levels of all non-mortgage household debt and finds that charge-offs do not completely explain the decline in household debt balances, and that a change in consumer demand for credit has indeed taken place.[27] The estimates in Table 2 are consistent with this finding.

Table 2. Credit Card Debt Charged-Off and Net New Borrowing, 2005-2010

Year/ Quarter	Charge-Off Rate (Annualized)	Debt Outstanding	Implied Charge-Off Losses	Actual Change in Debt Balance	Implied Net New Borrowing
	Percentage		(Millions of Dollars)		
2005 Q1	4.63	804,364	-9,311	4,864	14,175
2005 Q2	4.36	814,254	-8,875	9,890	18,765
2005 Q3	4.46	819,758	-9,140	5,504	14,644
2005 Q4	5.96	829,576	-12,361	9,818	22,179
2006 Q1	3.12	836,905	-6,528	7,329	13,856
2006 Q2	3.48	847,812	-7,376	10,908	18,284
2006 Q3	3.92	856,894	-8,398	9,081	17,479
2006 Q4	4.07	870,998	-8,862	14,105	22,967
2007 Q1	3.95	885,555	-8,745	14,556	23,301
2007 Q2	3.70	904,034	-8,362	18,479	26,841
2007 Q3	4.04	921,409	-9,306	17,375	26,682
2007 Q4	4.34	941,825	-10,219	20,416	30,635
2008 Q1	4.75	960,322	-11,404	18,497	29,901
2008 Q2	5.19	969,687	-12,582	9,365	21,947
2008 Q3	5.56	973,470	-13,531	3,783	17,314
2008 Q4	6.64	957,547	-15,895	-15,923	-28
2009 Q1	7.71	936,284	-18,047	-21,262	-3,216
2009 Q2	9.34	914,960	-21,364	-21,325	40
2009 Q3	10.03	893,510	-22,405	-21,450	955
2009 Q4	9.85	865,848	-21,322	-27,662	-6,341
2010 Q1	10.25	840,702	-21,543	-25,145	-3,602
2010 Q2	10.37	825,399	-21,398	-15,303	6,096
2010 Q3	8.39	806,089	-16,908	-19,310	-2,402
2010 Q4	7.70	799,706	-15,394	-6,383	9,011

Source: Federal Reserve, Charge-Off and Delinquency Rates on Loans and Leases at Commercial Banks, and Consumer Credit (Release G.19), and CRS estimates.

A reduction in new credit card borrowing may be either a supply or a demand effect. That is, consumers may be reducing their credit card use voluntarily or lenders may be restricting access to credit card borrowing. Some information on this question is available from recent surveys and panel studies by regional Federal Reserve banks.

On the supply side, there is evidence that lenders have taken steps to protect themselves against an unwanted surge in credit card loan balances, which represent risky unsecured assets against which capital must be held. According to the New York Fed study cited above, many credit card accounts have been closed by lenders, resulting in a 28% decrease in the limit on credit card borrowing.[28] Most of the accounts closed, however, appear to have been inactive—in other words, lenders may wish to prevent a future expansion of risky borrowing, but not to the point they drive active customers to their competitors. A Philadelphia Fed study found that 70% of accounts closed through the first quarter of 2010 were dormant or inactive.[29]

On the demand side, the New York Fed researchers also reported that the number of new credit card accounts opened has fallen sharply. This fact could indicate either that fewer consumers are applying for new credit cards or that lenders are rejecting more applications than in the past. To answer the question, the New York Fed study presents data showing that consumer requests for new accounts have fallen at about the same rate as new account openings, meaning that there is no strong evidence that tightening of credit standards has played a major role in reducing credit card debt outstanding.[30]

Mortgage Deleveraging

Figure 13 shows the quarter-to-quarter changes in home equity and other mortgage debt between 2005 and 2010. These Federal Reserve data suggest that the reduction in home equity balances (as a percentage of debt outstanding) has been much more dramatic than for mortgage debt in general. Between the beginning of the 2007-2008 recession and the fourth quarter of 2010, home equity debt fell by 16.1%, or $182 billion. Total mortgage debt, which includes home equity, fell by 4.4%, or $470 billion. Thus, despite accounting for only 10.8% of all mortgage debt at the end of 2007, home equity credit has accounted for 39% of the decline in household mortgage debt outstanding.[31]

Although increasing defaults and foreclosures caused mortgage loan charge-offs to rise sharply beginning in 2007, it is difficult to perform a charge-off analysis for mortgages comparable to the analysis of credit card debt in Table 2. A charged-off mortgage is not the same as a charged-off credit card loan. Credit card debt is unsecured—when a loan is written off, it simply ceases to exist. When a mortgage goes into default, on the other hand, the lender generally seizes the collateral—the house—and makes a new loan when the house is sold. Therefore, the amount of a mortgage that goes into default does not cause an equal reduction in the balance of mortgage debt outstanding, because the house will be resold (if at all possible)[32] and a new mortgage created.

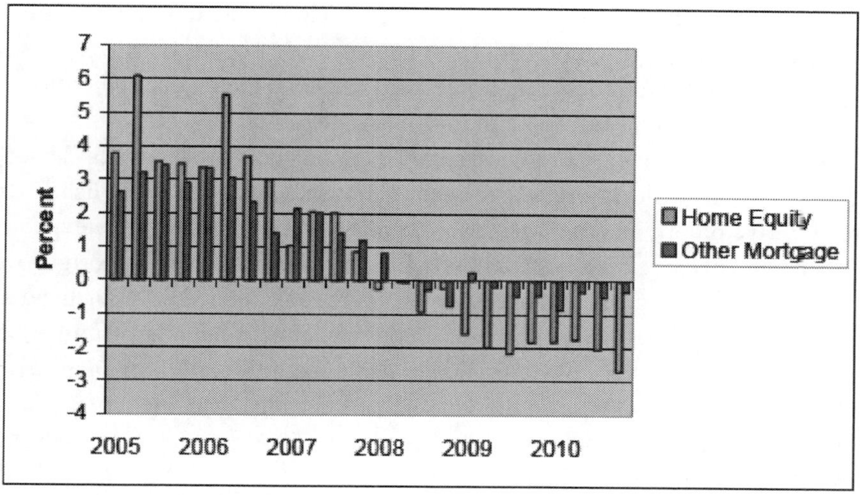

Source: Federal Reserve, *Flow of Funds Accounts*, Table L.218.

Figure 13. Quarterly Percentage Changes in Home Equity and Other Mortgage Debt Outstanding, 2005-2010.

In an environment of falling prices, defaults cause debt balances to fall, even when houses are resold, because most new mortgages are smaller than the retired mortgage on the same property. Loan modifications negotiated between lender and borrower may also reduce the mortgage principal outstanding, with the difference often charged off by the lender.[33]

Given that home equity lending may reflect borrowing for a wider variety of purposes other than financing a home purchase, this decline could be interpreted as a change in household debt use.

Home equity loans are used to consolidate existing debt obligations, finance new consumption, and finance the acquisition of new assets, while permitting homeowners to enjoy the taxdeductible benefits of mortgage debt. Consequently, many households made a substitution from other forms of credit to home equity credit. The interpretation of declining home equity debt as evidence of demand-side household deleveraging is not straightforward, however, given that lenders can both lower limits on existing lines of credit and reduce the amount of new home equity loans. This would be expected when the collateral securing the credit has declined or is expected to decline. According to the New York Fed, home equity borrowing limits fell by 12% through the third quarter of 2010, reflecting a tightening of supply.[34] At the same time, consumers would be expected to be more wary of home equity borrowing once house prices ceased to rise. Thus, whether the decline in aggregate home equity credit reflects a choice made by the borrower, which would be a fall in credit demand, or a choice made by the lender, which would be a fall in credit supply, is difficult to disentangle.

Another data series that sheds some light on the supply versus demand question deals with mortgage refinance transactions. Data published by Freddie Mac on refinances of prime conventional mortgages suggest evidence of changing behavior by both lenders and borrowers. When a mortgage is refinanced, the principal balance may be increased, reduced, or unchanged. During the mid-2000s housing boom, the overwhelming number of refinances resulted in the borrower converting some of the equity in the home into cash. This resulted in an increase in the amount of mortgage principal outstanding. When the loan balance increases by more than 5%, Freddie Mac calls the transaction a "cash-out" refinance.

Cash-out refinancings have become much less common, as Figure 14 shows. In Freddie Mac's analysis, both supply and demand factors are involved: "[t]he main causes of the decline in cashout refinancing were reduced home prices, tighter underwriting standards for loan-to-value ratios, and borrowers' desire to pay down debt."[35] As house prices began to fall, less home equity was available for cash-out purposes. Borrowers received $6.8 billion in cash-out transactions in the fourth quarter of 2010, compared with $83.6 billion at the peak of the boom in the second quarter of 2006.[36]

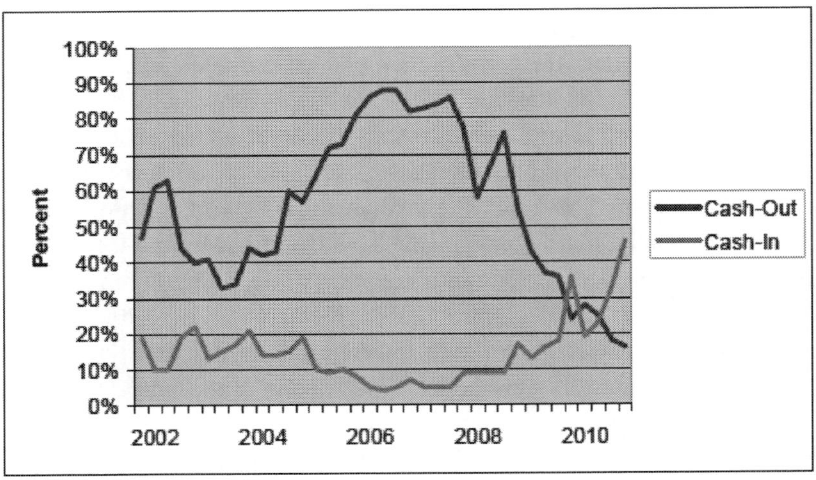

Source: Freddie Mac.

Note: The percentages do not add to 100 because refinances that do not change the amount of principal outstanding are not included.

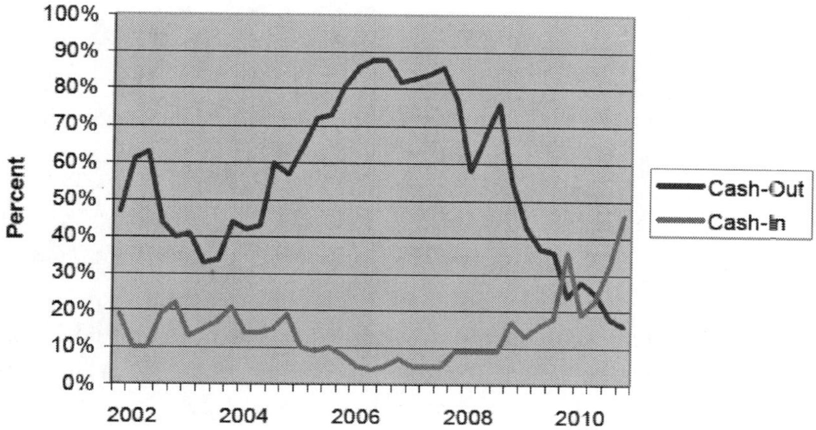

Source: Freddie Mac.

Note: The percentages do not add to 100 because refinances that do not change the amount of principal outstanding are not included.

Figure 14. Percentage of Mortgage Refinancings in which the Outstanding Balance Increases ("Cash-Out") or Decreases ("Cash-In"), 2002-2010.

A "cash-in" refinance, on the other hand, occurs when the borrower pays cash to reduce the amount of principal outstanding on the mortgage. These deals were relatively rare during the boom, but have become more common since 2008. During the second half of 2010, cash-in refinances exceeded cash-out deals as a percentage of all mortgage refinance transactions. The increase in cash-in deals suggests that a significant number of households are actively seeking to reduce their debt outstanding.

CONCLUSION

Data presented in this report suggest that there has been a significant, sustained reversal of the decades-long trend of rising household debt. From the aggregate debt figures, it is difficult to distinguish between several possible causal factors. But the available evidence suggests that reduced demand for borrowing, restrictions on the supply of credit, and a higher volume of loans charged-off have all contributed to falling debt balances.

Consumer borrowing, which outpaced income growth for many decades, may have finally hit an unsustainable level. A decline in net worth may have caused households to divert resources from consumption to savings and debt repayment. The fall in home prices provides incentives to default for homeowners who owe more than the market value of their house; other homeowners may default on other debt to avoid foreclosure. The phenomenon of falling house prices has not been observed on a national scale since the 1930s, which may help explain why recessions or asset bubbles previous to 2007 were not followed by deleveraging.

Household deleveraging has important consequences for the economy. Deleveraging may constitute drag on the recovery, particularly on consumption growth. Weakened household balance sheet positions that translate into defaults subsequently weaken lender balance sheet positions. In addition, credit markets are likely to experience both (1) a decline in household demand and (2) a decline in the supply of new loans while both groups work toward repairing weakened balance sheets. Furthermore, slower consumption growth dampens business investment, which exacerbates the problems of idle capacity in productive resources and substantial unemployment.

As the 112th Congress weighs strategies to create jobs, fiscal policy measures designed to stimulate household consumption may be less effective than in the past, while household balance sheets are in flux. Consequently, the level of employment may initially be more responsive to growth in two other components of demand—net exports and government spending—although policies designed to boost either component involve other sets of considerations that extend beyond purely macroeconomic factors.

Appendix. Deleveraging in the Great Depression

The last sustained, multi-year decline in U.S. household debt was during the Great Depression. Consumer credit and residential mortgage debt peaked in 1929 and fell until 1933. Debt balances did not regain 1929 levels until 1941.

Some difficulties attend comparisons between the current episode of deleveraging and the Depression, beginning with the definition of "consumer credit." Today the Federal Reserve divides consumer credit into two categories: revolving debt (primarily credit cards) and nonrevolving debt (primarily auto and education loans). In the 1930s, the Fed's data series on consumer credit was broken into installment and noninstallment credit outstanding.[37]

"Installment credit" consisted of all consumer credit that was scheduled to be repaid in two or more payments, including the following:

- automobile paper, credit extended to purchase new or used cars, whether or not the debt was secured by the vehicle;
- other consumer goods paper, to finance purchase of nonautomotive consumer goods, such as furniture, jewelry, boats, and appliances; and
- personal loans, made by financial institutions to individuals for consumer purposes.

"Noninstallment credit" was defined as debt scheduled to be repaid in a lump sum, including

- single-payment loans, made to individuals for consumer purposes, usually for meeting short-term needs, such as tax bills or insurance premiums rather than to finance consumption;
- charge accounts, or debt owed to retailers for purchases made by consumers, generally payable in full within 30 days of billing; and
- service credit, or amounts owed by individuals to professionals or service establishments. The largest components were medical and public utility bills.

In 1929, installment credit stood at $3.5 billion, noninstallment at $3.6 billion. The subsequent decline in installment credit was steeper: it fell to $1.7 billion in 1933, versus $2.2 billion for noninstallment credit.

The lists above suggest that there are some similarities between today's consumer credit markets and those of the Depression, but also major differences. A key distinction is that banks appear to have taken on a much greater intermediary role: open-ended credit card loans substitute for several classes of 1930s debt owed directly to merchants and other nonfinancial establishments. Another difference is that the debt category called "charge accounts" is equivalent to credit card balances that are paid off before interest charges apply, which are not currently counted as debt. Another important difference is that there was price deflation during the 1930s, meaning that the real value of debt increased when the dollar amount remained constant.

With these caveats, Figure A-1 compares the run-up in debt from 1919 (the first year for which a consumer credit figure is available) through 1929 and the subsequent decline in debt balances with a comparable period beginning in 1997 (10 years before the current deleveraging began). An estimation of mortgage data before 1929 was necessary, because earlier data combine debt owed on "1-4 family structures" with mortgages for "multifamily, residential and commercial structures." To obtain a series more comparable to current data, which exclude multifamily and commercial buildings, the Congressional Research Service has assumed that the percentage of total mortgage debt accounted for by 1-4 family structures was the same during the period 1919-1928 as it was in the years between 1929 and 1935. That is, 1-4 family housing is assumed to account for 56.3% of all mortgage debt between 1919 and 1928, which was the average ratio that prevailed from 1929 to 1935.[38]

The estimated home mortgage debt figure is added to the Fed's consumer credit figures to produce a total household debt figure over the period 1919-1941. That series is indexed and compared in the chart to an index of the same data that appear in Figure 1.

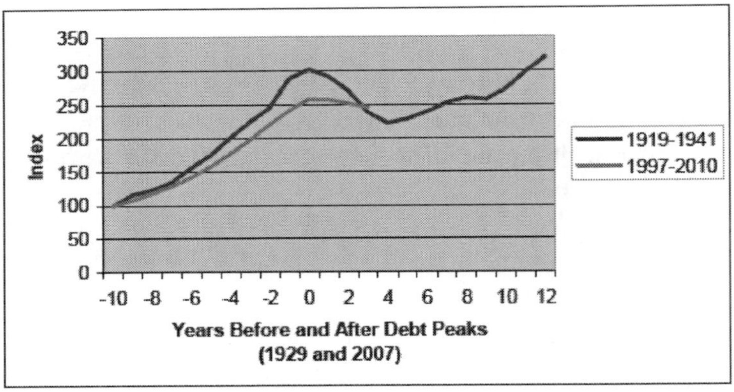

Source: U.S. Census Bureau, Historical Statistics of the United States and Federal Reserve, Flow of Funds Accounts (Release Z.1) and Consumer Credit (Release G. 19).

Notes: Index begins 10 years before the credit peaks, which occurred in 1929 and 2007.

Figure A-1. Household Debt Outstanding: Current Experience and the Great Depression, (Change in household debt balances).

Figure A-1 suggests that there were broad similarities in the magnitude of the run-up of household debt during the decade before deleveraging began, although the expansion of credit during the Roaring 20s was somewhat greater than what occurred post-1997. (Of course, the modern rise of debt did not begin in 1997.) On the other hand, the fall in debt balances during the 1930s was much more severe than what has been observed to date.

ACKNOWLEDGMENTS

The authors gratefully acknowledge the extensive and helpful comments of our colleagues in the Government and Finance Division, especially Mark Keightley, Linda Levine, and Ted Murphy.

End Notes

[1] See CRS Report R41434, *Job Growth During the Recovery*, by Linda Levine.

[2] Atif Mian and Amir Sufi, "Consumers and the Economy, Part II: Household Debt and the Weak U.S. Recovery," *Federal Reserve Bank of San Francisco Economic Letter* (2011-02), January 18, 2011.

[3] See CRS Report R41578, *Unemployment: Issues in the 112th Congress*, by Jane G. Gravelle, Thomas L. Hungerford, and Marc Labonte.

[4] Nonrevolving consumer credit also includes loans for boats, mobile homes, and other personal loans. Besides mortgages, revolving, and nonrevolving credit, the Federal Reserve calculates values for other forms of debt owed by households, including credit for securities bought on margin, but these appear to be less than 2% of the total. Figures for other debt are difficult to use because they include debts of non-profit organizations. See Federal Reserve, *Flow of Funds Accounts*, Table B.100.

[5] According to the National Bureau for Economic Research, the economy was in recession most recently (1) between July 1981 and July 1982, (2) between July 1990 and March 1991, (3) between March and November of 2001, and (4) between December 2007 and June 2009.

[6] That is, the value of debt outstanding during the period when each recession began is set equal to 100. The Federal Reserve Board reports revolving and nonrevolving consumer credit outstanding in monthly intervals and mortgage data in quarterly intervals.

[7] Consumer credit is reported monthly; mortgage debt quarterly.

[8] The 1990-1991 recession saw a sharp drop in automobile sales, and level of nonrevolving credit did not return to the pre-recession level until mid-1994. Automobile sales also dropped during the 2007-2009 recession, but the "cash-forclunkers" program may have offset some of the decline. See CRS Report R40654, *Accelerated Vehicle Retirement for Fuel Economy: Cash for Clunkers,* by Brent D. Yacobucci and Bill Canis. Continued growth in student lending may also have prevented a drop in nonrevolving credit outstanding.

[9] Reduced to its essentials, the debate that led to the enactment of the Bankruptcy Abuse Prevention and Consumer Protection Act of 2005 (BAPCPA; P.L. 109-8) consisted of two arguments: (1) that lenient bankruptcy laws led to excessive and/or abusive borrowing by consumers seeking to live beyond their means, and (2) that high rates of bankruptcy were an inevitable outcome of the marketing strategies of lenders, which snared unwary consumers.

[10] The Federal Reserve defines a household in "financial distress" as one that spends over 40% of its income on debt repayment. For related statistics, see CRS Report RS20777, *Consumer Bankruptcy and Household Debt*, by Mark Jickling and Jennifer Teefy.

[11] See Chapter Two, "Let Them Eat Credit," in: Raghuram Rajan, *Fault Lines: How Hidden Fractures Still Threaten the World Economy* (Princeton: Princeton University Press, 2010). Rajan argues that excessive consumer borrowing may have been encouraged by governments as a palliative for growing income inequality. For opposing views, see "Economics Focus: The Beautiful and the Damned," *Economist*, January 22, 2011, p. 90.

[12] See Reuven Glick and Kevin J. Lansing, "U.S. Household Deleveraging and Future Consumption Growth," *Federal Reserve Bank of San Francisco Economic Letter* (2009-16), May 15, 2009.

[13] Disposable personal income is the sum of employee compensation, proprietors' income, income from rent, interest and dividends, and government transfer payments, less income and payroll taxes.

[14] Between the end of 2006 and the first quarter of 2009, household sector holdings of corporate equities declined by $4.6 trillion, or 48%, whereas household real estate lost $5.2 trillion, or 27%. Federal Reserve, *Flow of Funds Accounts*, Table B.100.

[15] See Christopher D. Carroll, "Buffer-Stock Saving and the Life Cycle/Permanent Income Hypothesis," *Quarterly Journal of Economics*, vol. 112, no. 1 (February 1997), pp. 1-55 and Christopher D. Carroll, Karen E. Dynan, and Spencer D. Krane, "Unemployment Risk and Precautionary Wealth: Evidence from Households' Balance Sheets," *Review of Economics and Statistics*, vol. 85, no. 3 (2003), pp. 586-604.

[16] For a discussion of trigger events and the impact on delinquency and default behavior, see Darryl E. Getter, "Contributing to the Delinquency of Borrowers," *Journal of Consumer Affairs*, vol. 37 (2003), pp. 86-100.

[17] "New CoreLogic Data Shows Third Consecutive Quarterly Decline in Negative Equity," press release, December 13, 2010.

[18] See CRS Report R40210, *Preserving Homeownership: Foreclosure Prevention Initiatives*, by Katie Jones for foreclosure data.

[19] Expectations of stock volatility may also mean that households are less likely to increase their spending and borrowing when stock prices rise sharply than they are during a housing boom.

[20] Recent research suggests that consumer spending decisions are more closely linked to changes in the value of real estate assets than is the case with financial assets. See John D. Benjamin, Peter Chinloy, and G. Donald Jud, "Real Estate Versus Financial Wealth in Consumption," *Journal of Real Estate Finance and Economics*, vol. 29, no. 3 (2004), pp. 341-354 and Nathalie Girouard and Sveinbjörn Blöndal, *House Prices and Economic Activity*, OECD Economics Department Working Paper 279, January 2001.

[21] See http://www.federalreserve.gov/boarddocs/SnLoanSurvey/default.htm.

[22] For an attempt to construct a long term credit supply series from loan officer survey data, see Reuven Glick and Kevin J. Lansing, "Consumers and the Economy, Part I: Household Credit and Personal Saving," *Federal Reserve Bank of San Francisco Economic Letter* (2011-01), January 10, 2011.

[23] See Mark Whitehouse, "Defaults Account for Most of Pared Down Debt," *Wall Street Journal Online*, September 18, 2010, at http://blogs.wsj.com/economics/2010/09/18/number-of-the-week-defaults-account-for-most-of-pareddown- debt/ and Christine Hauser, "Bank Losses Lead to Drop in Credit Card Debt," *New York Times*, September 24, 2010.

[24] The "implied loss" is the value of debt outstanding times the charge-off rate for that quarter, divided by four (because the charge-off rates are annualized). The implied loss figure should be treated as an estimate because (1) actual loan charge-offs may not all occur in the same quarter, and (2) the loss rate figures are for commercial banks only, whereas the debt outstanding figures cover all credit card lenders.

[25] This is simply the difference between the current debt level and the previous quarter's figure.

[26] It is calculated by subtracting charge-offs from the actual change in debt outstanding. Thus, if there were no chargeoffs, the change in debt balance would be equal to net new borrowing. If net new borrowing does not change, chargeoffs will account for the entire change in debt balances.

[27] See Meta Brown, Andrew Haughwout, and Donghoon Lee, *The Financial Crisis at the Kitchen Table: Trends in the Household Debt and Credit*, Federal Reserve Bank of New York, Staff Reports 480, New York, NY, December 2010, http://www.ny.frb.org/research/staff_reports/sr480.html.

[28] Ibid., p. 8.

[29] Susan Herbst-Murphy, "Trends and Preferences in Consumer Payments: Lessons from the Visa Payment Panel Study," Payment Cards Discussion Paper, May 2010, p. 3.

[30] Meta Brown et al., "The Financial Crisis at the Kitchen Table," p. 7.

[31] Federal Reserve, *Flow of Funds Accounts*, Table L.218.

[32] Houses may not be sold as quickly as lenders would like, and the inventory of unsold homes climbed sharply during the crisis. The aggregate debt balance reflects new mortgages once these properties are sold. For data on unsold housing inventory, see CoreLogic, *U.S. Housing and Mortgage Trends*, November 2010, at http://www.corelogic.com/uploadedFiles/Pages/About_Us/ResearchTrends/US_Housing_and_Mortgage_Trends_1110.pdf.

[33] For information on mortgage modification programs, see CRS Report R40210, *Preserving Homeownership: Foreclosure Prevention Initiatives*, by Katie Jones.

[34] Meta Brown et al., "The Financial Crisis at the Kitchen Table," p. 8.

35 See Freddie Mac, "46 Percent of Refinancing Homeowners Pay Down Debt in Fourth Quarter: Share of Refinancers Who Take Cash Out At Record Low, Press Release, Jan. 31, 2011. Online at http://www.freddiemac.com/news/ archives/rates/2011/4qupb10.html.

[36] Ibid.

[37] U.S. Census Bureau, *Historical Statistics of the United States: Bicentennial Edition*, 1975, part 2, p. 1000. All the Depression-era data in this Appendix are from this source.

[38] Between 1929 and 1935 the ratio of 1-4 family to all residential mortgages varied between 57.7% and 54.5%.

In: Savings Shifts in America
Editor: Constantina Azzarà

ISBN: 978-1-61470-392-1

Chapter 2

SAVING RATES IN THE UNITED STATES: CALCULATION AND COMPARISON*

Craig K. Elwell

SUMMARY

The amount of money saved has important economic consequences. Nationally, the amount of saving affects how much can be invested and ultimately the size of the capital stock. Increasing the size of the capital stock is believed to be one way to raise the productivity of the labor force and the economy's long-term growth rate. Individually, saving is critical to accumulating sufficient wealth to maintain living standards after retirement. This report explains how national saving is measured, presents recent estimates of saving rates in the United States, and, for comparison, provides those of other major industrial countries.

The pace of economic growth is likely to be a matter of particular importance in the decades just ahead as the economy confronts the need to effect unprecedented generational transfers of income to pay for the retirement of the baby-boom generation. A larger economic pie makes such transfers easier for the economy to bear. Because the national rate of saving has implications for the pace of economic growth and the country's capacity to meet these long-term obligations, it is likely to be matter of ongoing concern to Congress.

* This is an edited, reformatted and augmented version of a Congressional Research Service publication, CRS Report for Congress RS21480, from www.crs.gov, dated September 14, 2010.

Introduction

Anyone with income and a future must decide how much to spend and how much to save. Individuals may save a fraction of their income for precautionary reasons, as well as to provide for themselves in retirement. Businesses retain a fraction of their profits in order to finance new investments. Governments save (or dis-save) as a consequence of policy decisions about how much to tax and how much to spend.

The amount of money saved as a nation has important economic consequences. If individuals save too little during their working lives to avoid falling living standards in old age, that may influence policymakers' views about the appropriate level of Social Security taxes and benefits. National saving, the sum of individual, business, and public saving, has important consequences for the balance of trade, economic growth, and future standards of living.[1]

Although economic theory gives no reason to prefer one saving rate over another, it may still be useful to examine trends in saving and to compare U.S. saving rates with those in other countries. This report provides a brief explanation of how saving is measured, and it provides current data on saving rates in the United States and for selected foreign countries.

Measuring Saving

Saving, in a nutshell, is after-tax income minus consumption. In an economic sense, however, consumption is not the same as expenditures. Translating the theoretical notion of saving into a statistical measure is a challenge.

The source for U.S. saving data is the national income and product accounts (NIPA) published by the Department of Commerce, Bureau of Economic Analysis (BEA). The NIPA constitute the accounting framework which is used to produce estimates of gross domestic product (GDP). GDP is the total value of goods and services produced, and it can be calculated in two different ways. One way is to add up the value of all the goods and services produced (the product side of the accounts), and the other way is to add up all of the income earned in the production of those goods and services (the income side of the account).

On the product side, GDP is the total value of those goods and services produced for personal consumption (C), investment (I), government (G), as well as for export (X). On the income side, the income earned in the production of those goods and services can be accounted for as consumer spending (C), taxes (T), private saving (S), and spending for imported goods and services (M).

Since each of these approaches measure the same variable (GDP), they can be set equal to each other, in this way:

$$C + I + G + X = C + T + S + M$$

Subtracting consumption (C) from both sides simplifies the equality:

$$I + G + X = T + S + M$$

This can now be rearranged by subtracting government spending (G) and exports (X) from both sides, which gives:

$$I = S + (T - G) + (M - X)$$

This equation illustrates the importance of saving. Total investment is equal to the sum of private saving (S), public saving (T-G), and the net inflow of capital from abroad (M-X).[2]

Gross and Net Saving

In the broadest sense, saving is income less consumption. Consumption is typically taken to mean spending on goods and services by households. But consumption can also refer to the wear and tear (depreciation, or capital consumption) on the capital stock that occurs in the production of those goods and services. Thus, some saving must be allocated to the replacement of the existing capital stock as it wears out. Only if saving is more than sufficient to replace the existing capital stock as it wears out can the capital stock grow.

For this reason, saving data distinguish between "gross" and "net" saving. The difference between the two measures is the estimated deterioration in the existing capital stock. In some cases, such as computers, capital may be completely depreciated in a very short period of time, whereas in others, such as buildings or heavy equipment, capital may take a long time to wear out.

Saving and Economic Growth

Economic growth, in the long run, is determined by three factors: the growth rate of the labor force; the rate of technological progress; and the rate of growth of the capital stock. The productivity of the labor force depends on both the level of technology and the size of the capital stock. The more capital there is, the more productive the labor force can be. The size of the capital stock, in turn, depends on the rate of investment.

Investment is directly related to saving. Saving more can lead to increased investment, resulting in a larger stock of capital and higher levels of productivity. Consuming less now enables more consumption in the future.

Thrift is considered by many to be a virtue, but economic theory gives no reason to prefer one saving rate over another. The amount saved is seen simply as a reflection of the trade-off made between a desire to consume now and a willingness to consume less than one's current income to provide resources for the future.

Historical Saving Data

Table 1 presents historical estimates of U.S. saving rates since 2000. The data in the top third of the table relate to the contribution of the private sector (personal or household saving, and business saving) to national saving, followed by data indicating the saving of the public sector, with separate accounting for the federal and state and local (S&L) government. The bottom third of the table shows both total gross and net national saving, the amount of saving imported from abroad, and total investment as a percentage of gross domestic product.

The U.S. gross personal saving rate had averaged about 7% of GDP through the 1960s, 1970s, and 1980s. In the 1990s, the personal saving rate decreased, averaging about 4.5% of GDP. In the 2000s, the personal saving rate continued to fall, reaching a low of 1.1% by 2005.[3] It is likely that the evaporation of household saving over the past two decades was in large measure a consequence of the sizable increase in household net worth associated with increased house and stock prices occurring at that time. Substantial increases in household wealth made it less urgent to divert current income to saving. However, the sharp reduction of household net worth during the recent recession dramatically changed the financial circumstances of households, reducing the use of debt-financed spending. The need to repair household balance sheets is likely to induce households to increase their rate of saving and to pay down debt. The poor prospect for the appreciation of house prices will sharply limit the ability to use rising equity as a substitute for saving. As the economic decline intensified, the personal saving rate increased, climbing to 2.0% in 2008 and 6.7% in 2009.[4]

The financial imperatives behind greater personal saving are going to persist for some time, and with the recovery of household income the ability to save will also improve, suggesting that the personal saving rate could continue to increase for several more years.

The U.S. gross public (government) saving rate has been negative for most of the past three decades because of persistent federal government budget deficits. The recent recession has caused federal budget deficits to increase sharply, reducing public saving accordingly (making it more negative) in 2008 and 2009. The recent large increases in federal budget deficits reflect changes in fiscal policy to stimulate aggregate demand in an effort to counter the recession and support an economic recovery. Those policy changes occurred partly through the action of "automatic stabilizers" that occur without deliberative action, such as falling tax revenue and rising spending for unemployment benefits, and partly through discretionary fiscal stimulus measures, such as the American Recovery and Reinvestment Act of 2009 (P.L. 111-5).

With economic recovery, the public saving rate is likely to increase as the automatic stabilizers work in the opposite direction and as the one-off stimulative spending runs its course. However, pending some resolution of the long-term budget problem of rising government spending for entitlements, public saving is likely to remain negative over the medium-term.

The U.S. gross business saving rate has historically been relatively stable, typically as a percentage of GDP staying within a range of 12% to 14%. This steadiness is largely attributable to the large capital consumption component (depreciation) of business saving, which is relatively insensitive to the ups and downs of the business cycle. The second and smaller component of business saving is undistributed profits (retained earnings). Undistributed profits are affected by the business cycle; nevertheless, such saving flows do not fluctuate widely and rebound quickly with economic recovery.

Table 1. Accounting for Saving in the United States (all figures as a percentage of gross domestic product)

	2000	2001	2002	2003	2004	2005	2006	2007	2008	2009
Gross Personal saving	2.1	2.0	2.7	2.6	2.6	1.1	2.1	1.3	2.0	6.7
Gross Business saving	11.7	12.3	12.9	13.0	13.4	14.1	16.0	12.7	13.3	13.7
Private Capital Consumption	9.9	10.2	10.3	10.2	10.1	10.2	12.2	10.4	10.6	10.8
Gross Private Saving	13.8	14.3	15.6	15.6	16.0	15.1	18.0	14.0	15.2	17.0
Net Private Saving	3.9	4.0	5.3	5.4	5.8	4.9	5.8	3.6	4.6	6.2
Gross Federal Saving	2.7	1.3	-1.5	-2.6	-2.4	-1.4	-0.9	-0.9	-3.6	-7.7
Federal Capital Consumption	0.9	0.9	0.8	0.8	0.8	0.8	0.9	0.8	0.8	0.9
Net Federal Saving	1.9	0.4	-2.4	-3.4	-3.2	-2.2	-1.8	-1.7	-4.4	-8.6
S&L Government Saving	1.5	1.0	0.6	0.8	1.1	1.4	1.9	1.4	1.0	1.3
S&L Capital Consumption	1.1	1.1	1.1	1.1	1.2	1.2	1.4	1.3	1.3	1.4
Net S&L Saving	0.4	-0.2	-0.5	-0.3	-0.1	0.2	0.4	0.2	-0.3	-0.1
Gross Public Saving	4.3	2.2	-0.9	-1.8	-1.3	-0.1	1.0	0.5	-2.6	-6.4
Net Public Saving	2.3	0.2	-2.9	-3.7	-3.3	-2.0	-1.3	-1.5	-4.7	-8.7
Gross National Saving	18.1	16.5	14.7	13.9	14.5	15.1	19.1	14.5	12.6	10.6
Net National Saving	6.2	4.3	2.4	1.8	2.5	2.9	4.5	2.0	-0.2	-2.5
Net Foreign Investment	4.1	3.8	4.2	4.6	5.3	5.9	7.0	5.1	4.9	3.0
Total Gross Domestic Investment	22.2	20.3	18.9	18.6	19.8	20.9	26.1	19.6	17.5	13.6

Source: Department of Commerce, Bureau of Economic Analysis.

Net foreign investment is a measure of inflows of foreign saving into the United States. Because domestic saving has persistently been insufficient to fully finance domestic investment, the United States has attracted foreign saving to fill that shortfall. Inflows of foreign saving as a percentage of GDP reached a record high of 7.0% in 2006. Since then foreign inflows of saving have decreased due in part to the dampening effects of the recent recession.

If with economic recovery domestic saving does not rise above its pre-recession level, foreign inflows of saving are likely to again increase.

INTERNATIONAL COMPARISONS

Just as it is sometimes argued that the saving rate is a matter for concern because it has fallen over time, it is argued that it is too low because it is below that of other countries. Table 2 presents data showing how national saving in the United States compares with that in other major industrial countries. These data differ somewhat from those presented in Table 1 because the Organization for Economic Co-operation and Development (OECD) uses a different set of economic accounting rules and because the OECD data are not revised on the same schedule as the NIPA data. The advantage of OECD data is that they are comparable across countries.

Table 2. Gross National Saving for Selected Countries (as a percentage of gross domestic product)

	United States	Canada	France	Germany	Italy	Japan	United Kingdom
1998	18.5	19.1	21.0	20.9	21.6	28.8	18.0
1999	17.9	20.7	21.8	20.3	21.1	27.2	15.7
2000	17.8	23.6	21.6	20.2	20.6	27.5	15.0
2001	16.2	22.2	21.3	19.5	20.9	25.8	15.4
2002	14.3	21.2	19.8	19.4	20.8	25.2	15.3
2003	13.5	21.4	19.1	19.5	19.8	25.4	15.1
2004	14.1	23.0	19.0	22.0	20.3	25.8	15.0
2005	14.6	23.8	18.5	22.1	19.5	26.8	14.6
2006	15.8	24.4	19.3	24.3	19.6	26.9	14.2
2007	14.0	23.7	19.9	26.3	20.0	27.0	15.5
2008	12.1	23.7	18.9	25.8	18.0	n.a.	15.4

Source: Organization for Economic Co-operation and Development.

Over the period shown, Japan saved at a higher rate than any of the other countries, although its saving rate has been falling. The United Kingdom and the U.S. saving rates were the lowest of these seven countries.

Table 3 presents data comparing historical household saving rates for the same countries. The OECD household saving data are based on the most recent internationally comparable data, but are available only as a percentage of disposable household income rather than as a percentage of GDP.

Table 3. Household Saving for Selected Countries (as a percentage of disposable income)

	United States	Canada	France[a]	Germany	Italy	Japan	United Kingdom[a]
1998	5.3	4.9	12.4	10.1	11.4	11.3	7.4
1999	3.1	4.0	12.1	9.5	10.2	10.0	5.2
2000	2.9	4.7	11.9	9.2	8.4	8.6	4.7
2001	2.7	5.2	12.7	9.4	10.5	5.0	6.0
2002	3.5	3.5	13.9	9.9	11.2	4.9	4.8
2003	3.5	2.6	12.6	10.3	10.3	3.9	5.1
2004	3.4	3.2	12.6	10.4	10.2	3.5	3.7
2005	1.4	2.1	11.7	10.5	9.9	3.9	3.9
2006	2.4	3.5	11.6	10.5	9.1	3.8	2.9
2007	1.7	2.5	12.2	10.8	8.2	3.3	2.2
2008	2.7	3.7	11.8	11.2	8.6	2.7	1.7
2009	4.3	5.0	16.3	11.3	8.4	2.3	7.0

Source: Organization for Economic Co-operation and Development.

[a.] France and the United Kingdom report gross saving, the others are net saving rates.

Acknowledgments

An earlier version of this report was authored by Brian Cashell.

End Notes

[1] For a discussion of public policy and saving, see CRS Report RL32119, *Can Public Policy Raise the Saving Rate?*, by Brian W. Cashell.

[2] Just as there is a balance between the income and product sides of the NIPA, there is a balance in international payments. If Americans buy more goods and services from abroad than they export, then (at least in this simplified example) the net outflow of dollars will be used by foreigners to buy dollar-denominated assets, which thus helps to finance domestic investment.

[3] See CRS Report R40647, *The Fall and Rise of Household Saving*, by Brian W. Cashell.

[4] U.S. Department of Commerce, Bureau of Economic Analysis, *National Accounts*, Table 5.1, http://www.bea.gov/ national/nipaweb/SelectTable.asp?Selected=N.

In: Savings Shifts in America
Editor: Constantina Azzarà

ISBN: 978-1-61470-392-1

Chapter 3

The Fall and Rise of Household Saving*

Brian W. Cashell

Summary

Household saving matters for two reasons. First, it is an important source of funds to finance domestic investment. Second, it is the means by which workers accumulate wealth and maintain their living standard into retirement. Congress has indicated its desire to promote household saving by, among other things, creating individual retirement accounts, and saving is an important consideration in proposals to reform Social Security. At a time, however, when policymakers have been looking for ways to increase spending to minimize the downturn and get the economy growing again, households have begun to save more.

For the 40 months between January 2005 and April 2008, the personal saving rate averaged 1.8%. In contrast, in the 1970s, the average personal saving rate was 9.6%. In May 2008, the personal saving rate began to rise. It remains too early to tell with certainty if that represents the reversal of the long-term decline. What may seem unusual is that it occurred at a time of general economic weakness. The increase in household saving resulted in more than $300 billion less in consumer spending than would have occurred had the saving rate not risen.

---

* This is an edited, reformatted and augmented version of a Congressional Research Service publication, CRS Report for Congress R40647, from www.crs.gov, dated September 1, 2009.

Prudent individuals might be expected to save enough to avoid a substantial decline in their living standard on retirement. If consumers seek to maintain a fairly stable level of consumption over their entire lives, then the level of consumption at any given point in their lives will depend on their current wealth and some expectation about their income over the rest of their lives.

Changes in household net worth in recent years seem to have contributed to the swings in the household saving rate. In the 1990s, equity prices rose substantially. Between 1991, the beginning of an economic expansion, and 2001, the year it ended, the Standard and Poor's index of 500 stock prices rose by 217%. It is widely believed those increases in equity prices contributed to a decline in the household saving rate.

After the turn of the century, increased house prices insulated household balance sheets from the effects of a decline in equity values, and the household saving rate fell to near zero.

More recently, both equity and house prices have fallen. The combined drop in asset prices had a significant effect on household net worth. At a time when current incomes have been falling, the personal saving rate rose to more than 5%. It may be that the economic downturn is limiting the saving response to the decline in household net worth. If that is the case, the saving rate might be expected to continue to rise, or at least remain steady at current levels, when the economy begins to recover, unless asset prices recover to levels now considered by many to have constituted a "bubble."

INTRODUCTION

In the 1970s, the average personal saving rate was 9.6%. At one time, in 2005, it was less than 1%. For the 40 months between January 2005 and April 2008, the personal saving rate averaged 1.8%. That it was so low for an extended period of time would seem to be cause for worry. In the past, Congress has indicated a desire to promote household saving by, among other things, creating individual retirement accounts, and saving is an important consideration in proposals to reform Social Security.

In May 2008, the personal saving rate began to rise. It is too early to tell with any certainty whether that represents the reversal of the long-term decline.

What may seem unusual is that the recent rise in household saving occurred at a time of general economic weakness. While policymakers hope to stimulate aggregate demand with an expansionary fiscal policy, the increase in household saving resulted in more than $300 billion less in consumer spending than would have occurred had the saving rate not risen.

Household saving is important for at least two reasons. First, most households must accumulate wealth over the course of their working lives if they are to avoid a decline in their standard of living after retiring. A negligible rate of saving might seem unlikely to afford a comfortable retirement for many, especially if Social Security benefits are ever reduced as part of any reform plan, as many workers fear may occur. Second, household saving is an important source of funds to finance capital investment, increasing the capital stock and adding to worker productivity.

People save for a variety of reasons. In addition to retirement saving, they save to provide for the proverbial rainy day, and this is sometimes referred to as "precautionary" saving. That day seems to have come, with incomes stagnant or falling and the unemployment rate rising, and households might be expected to save less in an effort to maintain their standard of living. But at the same time, asset prices have been falling, pushing down household net worth, which might be expected to prompt households to save more. At a time when the federal government is trying to use policy to stimulate spending to revive the economy, households have cut back their spending by more than the drop in income.

This report begins by showing how the household saving rate has varied in recent years. Next, it explains how household saving is measured, and it provides some detail on how saving varies across the income distribution. Finally, it discusses factors that may account for the long decline in household saving, as well as prospects for its recovery.[1]

IS THE LONG-TERM DECLINE IN HOUSEHOLD SAVING OVER?

Beginning in the mid-1980s, the personal, or household, saving rate fell from close to 10% to less than 1% in 2005. Figure 1 shows the monthly personal saving rate since 1970.

The decline in the personal saving rate was persistent and pronounced, but some see signs of a recent reversal in that long downward trend. To understand what has happened, it is important first to explain what this measure of saving takes into account. As is the case with many economic statistics, there are differences between the theoretical notion of saving and the results of statistical efforts to measure it.

Source: Department of Commerce, Bureau of Economic Analysis.
Note: Data are four-month moving averages.

Figure 1. Personal Saving as a Percentage of Disposable Personal Income.

MEASURING SAVING

The simplest definition of saving is income minus consumption. What is not spent is saved. In practice, however, what counts as income and how to measure consumption is not necessarily straightforward. The national income and product accounts (NIPA) published by the Bureau of Economic Analysis (BEA) of the Department of Commerce are the primary source for statistics on overall U.S. economic activity.[2] The aim of the NIPA is to account for both income and expenditures that are related to the current production of goods and services. Changes in asset values are not included since they have nothing to do with current production. Thus, capital gains and losses are not counted as income in the NIPA.

Even though capital gains are not included in the NIPA measure of personal income, they still affect the measurement of the personal saving rate. Tax payments on capital gains realizations are included in personal tax payments. Thus, after-tax personal income is reduced by the amount of the tax payments. Personal (or household) saving, which is calculated by subtracting consumption from (after-tax) income, is reduced as well.

The NIPA measure of saving differs from saving in the theoretical sense in its treatment of consumer durable goods.[3] Ideally, the consumption of durable goods would be measured by the value of the flow of services they provide over their useful lives, similar to an investment. In the NIPA, however, consumption of durable goods is treated like any other type of consumer spending, by simply counting the expenditures on those goods.

A similar difference occurs with respect to expenditures on education. They are treated in the NIPA as consumption spending, but given that they yield benefits over an individual's lifetime they might more appropriately be counted as investment spending. If they were, that would raise the measured saving rate.

If the actual measure of saving more closely approximated the theoretical measure it would likely be higher but unless the difference between the theoretical and actual measure has changed significantly, it would still show a trend decline since the 1980s.

An Alternative Measure

The Board of Governors of the Federal Reserve Board (Fed) publishes an estimate of household saving that differs somewhat from the one published by BEA. The BEA estimate of household saving is calculated by subtracting consumption expenditures from income. In contrast, the Fed estimate is based on a balance sheet for the household sector. When households save, it shows up in the Fed's flow of funds accounts as an increase in household net worth. The gross increase in household net worth is the sum of the net acquisition of financial and tangible assets minus the net increase in household liabilities. The Fed publishes two estimates of household saving; one that includes net investment in durable goods (mostly automobiles) and one that does not. The one that does not is conceptually equivalent to the BEA measure of saving.

Figure 2 shows the household saving rate from the flow of funds accounts including the net increase in household durable goods. The alternative Fed measure shows the same steady decline as the BEA measure. But instead of falling from about 10% to less than 1%, the Fed measure shows a decline from more than 14% in the 1970s to about zero. The Fed measure of the household saving rate suggests a similar rebound beginning in 2008.

Accounting for net investment in consumer durables as saving is arguably appropriate, given that saving is defined as income less consumption. But when policymakers express concern about the low saving rate, the distinction between the Fed measure and the BEA measure may not make much difference. One public policy concern over low household saving relates to retirement saving, and investments in automobiles and household furnishings are not likely to be a source of money income for retirees. What is significant is that the independent measures both suggest that, the recent rebound notwithstanding, the household saving rate remains at relatively low historical levels.

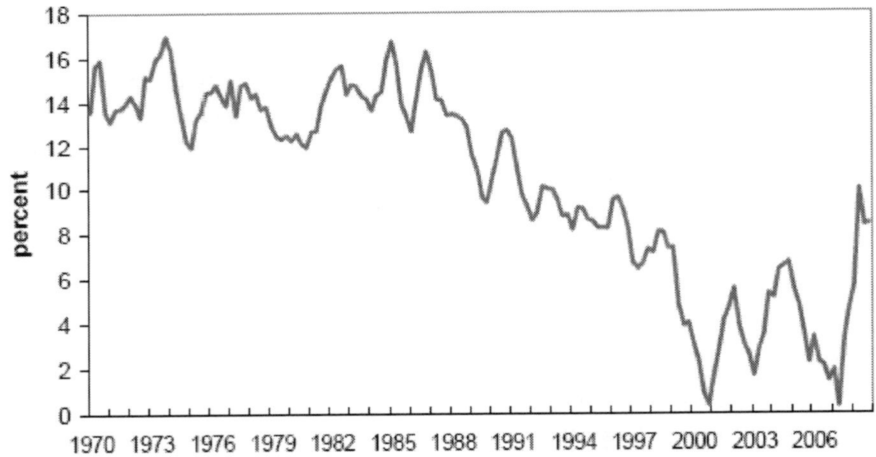

Source: Board of Governors of the Federal Reserve System.
Note: Data are four-quarter moving averages.

Figure 2. Flow of Funds Household Saving Rate.

HOUSEHOLD SAVING AND WEALTH ACCUMULATION

The standard model of consumer spending used in economic analysis assumes that consumers seek to avoid large swings in their living standards over the course of their lifetimes. Thus as incomes rise and fall both in the short and long term, individuals are expected to vary their saving rate in order to minimize the effect on their consumption.

Typically, over the course of an individual's lifetime, income has a tendency first to rise over the course of a career, and then fall in retirement.

The model of saving based on this "life cycle" presumes that, in order to dampen the effects of the lifetime income cycle on consumption and living standards, individuals vary the rate at which they save.[4] Saving will thus tend to be relatively higher during their peak earning years, and lower at the beginning of their careers and during retirement.[5]

From an economic perspective, there is no "ideal" saving rate. The rate at which an individual saves is, for the most part, simply a reflection of his willingness to consume less now in order to be able to consume more in the future. Taking the life cycle model as a guide, however, prudent individuals might be expected to save enough to avoid a substantial decline in their living standard on retirement.

If consumers seek to maintain a fairly stable level of consumption over their entire lives, then the level of consumption at any given point in their lives will depend on their current wealth and some expectation about their income over the rest of their lives.[6]

A number of implications follow from this model of consumer behavior. One is that an unexpected one-time income windfall is more likely to be saved than spent. A rise in income that is temporary is less likely to raise consumption than one that is permanent as long as consumers seek to maintain a relatively constant standard of living. A permanent increase in income is more likely to induce an increase in consumption, so that the saving rate will be less affected. Similarly, an increase in overall wealth raises consumption possibilities over the long run. An increase in wealth is likely to reduce the measured rate of saving.

Consumption is ultimately constrained by income and wealth. An increase in wealth increases potential lifetime consumption and diminishes an individual's incentive to save. The effect of an increase in wealth on consumption and saving may depend on a number of variables Most important, if the life cycle model is correct, only a fraction of any increase in wealth would affect current consumption because any rise in consumption would be spread out over one's remaining lifetime. Some increases in wealth may not be viewed as permanent as might be the case with assets whose prices tend to be highly variable. If there is uncertainty about the permanence of an increase in wealth then it is less likely to affect consumption and saving. In addition, a strong desire to leave a bequest may dampen the influence increasing wealth has on consumption. The effect works in both directions. A decline in wealth is likely to result in a drop in consumption and an increase in saving, other things being equal.

Numerous studies of wealth and consumer spending have been conducted. Empirical estimates of the magnitude of the effect of changes in wealth on consumption vary, but they tend to be fairly small. The estimates suggest that for each additional dollar of wealth, consumption spending might be expected to rise by some amount between one cent and seven cents.[7]

Asset Prices and Personal Saving

One of the most striking aspects of past three economic expansions has been the dramatic gains in asset prices. For example, between 1991, the beginning of one expansion, and 2001, the year it ended, the Standard and Poor's index of 500 stock prices rose by 217%, the Dow Jones Index rose by 247%, and the NASDAQ stock price index increased by 313%. Then, beginning in late 1997, the price of housing rose rapidly relative to prior years. Between late 1997 and late 2007, the house price index published by the Office of Federal Housing Enterprise Oversight (OFHEO) nearly doubled.[8]

Given the model of saving behavior described above, it might be reasonable to suppose that those increases in asset prices had something to do with the coincidental decline in the personal saving rate.

A number of studies have found that the decline in the personal saving rate was due at least in part to the rise in equity prices. Lusardi, Skinner, and Venti found that between one-half to two-thirds of the decline in the personal saving rate was attributable to the effect of wealth gains on consumption spending.[9] They also point out that because of rising equity prices, firms were able to reduce their contributions to defined benefit retirement plans and still keep those plans fully funded. Pension benefits could be paid out of the capital gains of the pension fund. That tended to reduce a component of personal income (employers' contributions to pension funds) without reducing consumption and thus contributed to the decline in the saving rate.

Maki and Palumbo analyzed the drop in saving of the 1990s and found that almost all of it could be attributed to the performance of the stock market.[10] Moreover, they found that those households with the highest incomes experienced the largest gains in wealth and also the largest declines in saving rates. They concluded that, between 1992 and 2000, almost all of the decline in the aggregate personal saving rate can be attributed to reduced saving of those households in the top 20% of the income distribution. They also found that the saving rate of those households in the bottom 40% of the income distribution actually rose over the same period.

Because capital gains can contribute just as much to a household's retirement nest egg as saving, it might be appropriate to include them in measures of retirement saving. After all, the aim of saving for retirement is to accumulate enough wealth to be able to continue, in retirement, the lifestyle to which one has become accustomed during one's working life. Gale and Sabelhaus have calculated what the saving rate might have been if capital gains were included in the current measure of personal saving.[11] They found that, after adjusting for inflation, household wealth rose at least as rapidly in the late 1990s as at any time since 1960.

The stock market cooled off in 2001, but an increase in housing prices that began in late 1997 may have contributed to a continued decline in household saving.

There has also been a number of studies attributing the drop in household saving to housing price appreciation. Belsky and Prakken found that in the long run, the effects on household saving of house and equity price variations were similar.[12] They also found that house price appreciation had a more immediate effect and that the effect of equity price appreciation took longer to be fully reflected in the saving rate. The authors suggested that may be because historically equity prices have been more volatile than house prices, and so households may be more confident in the durability of house price gains. The authors also indicated that the strong effect of the post-2000 boom in house prices may have been partly due to the simultaneous decline in interest rates, which encouraged homeowners to refinance as well as borrow. They left open the question of whether, in other circumstances, house price appreciation would have the same effect on household saving.

Benjamin, Chinloy, and Jud found that changes in real estate wealth had a greater effect on spending and saving than did variations in financial wealth.[13] The authors found that for each $1 increase in real estate wealth, household saving would fall by 8¢, while for each $1 increase in financial wealth household saving would fall by just 2¢. They suggest that the effect of variations in financial wealth might be smaller because much financial wealth is tied up in pension and insurance funds and gains are not easy to withdraw. They also point out that financial wealth is concentrated and that some financial asset holding may represent controlling interests in businesses and thus not be readily liquidated.

Muellbauer found the wealth effect of housing had changed over time. He argues that developments in capital markets, such as credit scoring and securitization, enhanced households' ability to tap into gains in home equity.[14] Prior to those changes, he estimated the wealth effect of housing to be very small. During the housing market boom, he estimated that households might have increased spending by six cents or seven cents for each dollar increase in home equity.

The Decline in Household Net Worth and the Recent Increase in the Saving Rate

After peaking in early 2007, house prices fell significantly. Between April 2007 and February 2008, the OFHEO house price index fell by nearly 10%. Stock prices reached a peak in mid-2007. Between May 2007 and May 2009, the S&P500 stock price index fell by more than 40%. The combined drop in asset prices had a significant effect on household balance sheets. Between the second quarter of 2007 and the fourth quarter of 2008, total household net worth fell by an estimated $12.9 trillion, a drop of 20%. Other things being equal, that might be expected to prompt households to cut spending and to save more out of current income to offset the decline in wealth. But with current income falling, it might also seem to be the proverbial rainy day when an increased share of consumption would be financed by reducing saving or drawing on existing wealth.

If the estimates are correct that consumption falls by about five cents for each dollar decline in wealth, then the drop in household net worth might have been expected to result in a decline in consumer spending of more than $600 billion. The increase in household saving since May 2008 amounted to about half of that. It may be that the economic downturn is limiting the saving response to the decline in household net worth. If that is the case, the saving rate might be expected to continue to rise, or at least not to fall, when the economy begins to recover, unless asset prices recover substantially.

The recent rise in the personal saving rate also coincided with tax rebates subsequent to the enactment of the 2008 economic stimulus (P.L. 110-85),[15] and some might suggest that the rebates had something to do with the rise in personal saving. The life cycle model would seem to suggest that a temporary tax cut is more likely to be saved than spent. Because it has little effect on the anticipated stream of lifetime income, it might seem unlikely that a temporary tax cut would have as large an effect on consumption as a permanent one.[16]

Some evidence suggests that the rebates were not saved but rather led to a significant increase in consumer spending, perhaps in part because they were targeted at lower-income households, which tend to save less of their income than those at the other end of the income distribution.[17] Broda and Parker examined household expenditures both before and after receipt of the tax rebates. They found an increase in spending which they attributed to the rebate. They found a larger increase in spending among lower-income and less wealthy households. They also found an increase in the share of overall spending at discount supercenters.

A study by the Federal Reserve Bank of San Francisco compared the current financial situation of U.S. households with that of Japanese households when stock and real estate prices declined sharply in Japan between 1989 and 1991.[18] The authors projected that if U.S. households reduce their debt-to-income ratio at roughly the same pace as Japanese households did then, the U.S. household saving rate would gradually rise to 10% by the end of 2018. That increase in the saving rate would mean about 0.75% slower annual growth in consumption spending than would occur if the saving rate held steady, slowing the recovery from the current downturn.

WHO SAVES?

The saving rates shown in Figure 1 and Figure 2 are averages. But not everyone saves at the same rate and it might be informative to have an idea of how saving rates vary across households, by income in particular. Table 1 presents data on saving by quintile of income. The lowest quintile represents the bottom 20% of the income distribution, the second quintile represents the second lowest 20% in the distribution, and so on. The figures in the first row show saving rates.[19]

They are derived from data from the 2007 Survey of Consumer Expenditures, published by the Bureau of Labor Statistics. The figures in the second row are taken from the 2007 Survey of Consumer Finances published by the Board of Governors of the Federal Reserve System.[20]

Both sets of numbers indicate that those at the upper end of the income distribution account for most saving. On average, they save at a higher rate than those lower in the distribution, and a larger proportion of them save.

Table 1. Saving by Income Quintile

	Income Quintile				
	Lowest	Second	Third	Fourth	Fifth
Saving as a percent of aftertax household income (2007)	-94.3	-13.6	6.0	18.2	35.9
Percentage of families that saved (2007)	33.7	45.1	57.8	66.8	78.9

Sources: Department of Labor, Bureau of Labor Statistics; Board of Governors of the Federal Reserve System.

Are Households Saving Enough?

Even if the decline in the saving rate could be explained, it does not answer the question of whether Americans are saving enough, or accumulating enough wealth, to avoid experiencing a decline in their living standard in retirement. One study attempted to estimate how much households need to set aside in order to maintain their living standards into retirement.[21] Using a retirement planning financial model and data from a survey of the financial status of households approaching retirement, the authors found that low-income households (those with incomes below $15,000) needed to save only about 1% of their income. But that assumed that there would be no cuts in Social Security benefits. The authors estimated that if Social Security benefits were to be cut by 30% 15 years into the future, the desired saving rate would rise to 6%.

Households that have higher incomes need to save at higher rates if they are to avoid a decline in their living standards on retirement, because Social Security benefits will account for a much smaller share of their retirement income. The desired saving rate for those households with incomes between $15,000 and $100,000 was about 14%, but rose to about 20% in the case where future Social Security benefits were to be cut.[22]

Another study examined data from the University of Michigan Health and Retirement Study (HRS) to see if households were saving enough to maintain their living standards at retirement.[23] The authors found that more than 80% of the households in the survey had accumulated enough wealth to avoid a drop in their standard of living, and that for many of those who had not, the shortfall was not large. Given the drop in household net worth since the time of that study, that estimate might now be lower.

CONCLUSION

The drop in personal saving that occurred over the past 25 years may not have been as dramatic as might first appear, at least with respect to retirement planning, for several reasons. The decline in personal saving coincided with large increases in equity values and housing wealth. When changes in personal wealth are taken into account, the decline in the official saving measure may have been more modest.

Changes in asset values work both ways. The decline in asset values over the past year seems to have inspired households to save more, even at a time when incomes are falling. It may be that households are saving enough for retirement, and the saving rate seems to have recovered somewhat. The increase in household saving, however, is likely to be more than offset by a large decrease in public sector saving.

The federal government surpluses of the late 1990s have reversed, and the outlook is for substantial federal budget deficits for some time to come. For the immediate future, the public sector saving rate is expected to be much lower than it was in the late 1990s. Without a substantial increase in private saving, either investment spending will fall, or the United States will have to attract increasing amounts of capital from abroad.

If foreigners were to reduce or stop their investments in the United States, then the decline in demand for U.S. financial assets would cause their prices to fall. Interest rates would rise, unless there is an offsetting increase in domestic saving. A rise in interest rates would be likely to result in a decline in domestic investment.

The recent increase in the household saving rate may have longer-run benefits, but in the short run, if the household saving rate continues to climb, it could have the effect of slowing the economic recovery, and further moderating the effectiveness of current or prospective fiscal stimulus measures.

End Notes

[1] For a complete accounting of saving in the United States, see CRS Report RS21430, *Saving Rates in the United States: Calculation and Comparison*, by Brian W. Cashell.

[2] This is the source for the data shown in Figure 1.

[3] Consumer durable goods include automobiles, furniture, and household equipment.

[4] Any explanation of consumer saving behavior must reconcile two seemingly contradictory observations. At any given time, cross-section data suggest that individuals with low

incomes tend to have low rates of saving, while those at the higher end of the income distribution tend to have relatively high rates of saving. That might suggest that as incomes rise over time, saving rates would also tend to rise. That has not been the case. Over the long run, saving rates have not increased as incomes have grown.

[5] The life cycle model only partly explains consumer behavior. For many households, consumption depends on current income, and those households do not smooth their consumption over the course of their lifetimes. See N. Gregory Mankiw, "The Savers-Spenders Theory of Fiscal Policy," *American Economic Review*, May 2000.

[6] To the extent that consumers can borrow against future income, that enhances their ability to maintain a fairly steady level of consumption over a long period of time.

[7] See Martha Starr-McCluer, "Stock Market Wealth and Consumer Spending," Finance and Economics Discussion Series, 1998-20, Board of Governors of the Federal Reserve System, April 1998. Also, Congressional Budget Office, *The Economic and Budget Outlook: An Update*, August 1998, p. 19.

[8] There are theoretical reasons to believe an increase in the value of houses might have less of an effect on household saving behavior than stock equity price appreciation. An increase in house prices increases the wealth of current homeowners, but it also increases the cost of housing. For renters, that might result in a reduction in saving in order to pay increased rents. For many homeowners, an increase in housing wealth may simply translate into an increase in consumption of housing, rather than spending more for other goods and services. In that case, an increase in housing prices would be unlikely to show up as a reduction in saving out of current income.

[9] Annamaria Lusardi, Jonathan Skinner, and Steven Venti, "Saving Puzzles and Saving Policies in the United States," National Bureau of Economic Research, Working Paper 8237, April 2001.

[10] Dean M. Maki and Michael G. Palumbo, "Disentangling the Wealth Effect: A Cohort Analysis of Household Saving in the 1990s," Board of Governors of the Federal Reserve System, Finance and Economics Discussion Series, 2001-21, April 2001.

[11] William G. Gale and John Sabelhaus, "The Savings Crisis: In the Eye of the Beholder?" *The Milken Institute Review*, Third Quarter 1999, pp. 46-56.

[12] Eric Belsky and Joel Prakken, "Housing's Impact on Wealth Accumulation, Wealth Distribution and Consumer Spending, "National Association of Realtors National Center for Real Estate Research, 2004, available at http://www.realtor.org/research/ncrer/rewealtheffect.

[13] John D. Benjamin, Peter Chinloy, and G. Donald Jud, "Real Estate Versus Financial Wealth in Consumption," *Journal of Real Estate Finance and Economics*, vol. 29, no. 3, 2004.

[14] John N. Muellbauer, "Housing, Credit and Consumer Expenditure," paper prepared for the Federal Reserve Bank of Kansas City's Jackson Hole Symposium, August 2007, available at http://www.kansascityfed.org/publicat/sympos/ 2007/PDF/2007.08.15.Muellbauer.pdf.

[15] CRS Report RS22850, *Tax Provisions of the 2008 Economic Stimulus Package*, coordinated by Jane G. Gravelle.

[16] It may be worth noting that to the extent that the tax cut is saved it represents a shift of saving from the federal government to households.

[17] Christian Broda and Jonathan Parker, "The Impact of the 2008 Tax Rebates on Consumer Spending: Preliminary Evidence," July 2008, available at http://www.voxeu.org/ index.php?q=node/1541.

[18] Reuven Glick and Kevin J. Lansing, "U.S. Household Deleveraging and Future Consumption Growth," Federal Reserve Bank of San Francisco *Economic Letter*, May 15, 2009, available at http://www.frbsf.org/publications/economics/letter/2009/el2009-16.pdf.

[19] These saving rates should not be taken as precise estimates. They are derived by subtracting expenditures from income as reported in a survey. If the estimates of income and expenditures are biased in opposite directions then there could be considerable error in the resulting saving estimate. To some, the extreme negative saving rates for households in the lowest income quintile suggest that they may be significantly under-reporting income. John M. Rogers and Maureen B. Gray, "CE Data: Quintiles of Income Versus Quintiles of Outlays," *Monthly Labor Review*, December 1994, available at http://stats.bls.gov/opub/mlr/1994/12/art4full.pdf.

[20] This survey is conducted every three years. See the survey Web page at http://www.federalreserve.gov/pubs/oss/ oss2/scfindex.html.

[21] B. Douglas Bernheim, Lorenzo Forni, Jagadeesh Gokhale, and Laurence J. Kotlikoff, "How Much Should Americans Be Saving for Retirement?," Federal Reserve Bank of Cleveland Working Paper 00-02, January 1999, available at http://www.clevelandfed.org/Research/workpaper/2000/Wp0002.pdf.

[22] Ibid, p. 9.

[23] John Karl Scholz, Ananth Seshadri, and Surachai Khitatrakun, "Are Americans Saving "Optimally" for Retirement?," *Journal of Political Economy*, 2006:4.

In: Savings Shifts in America
Editor: Constantina Azzarà
ISBN: 978-1-61470-392-1

Chapter 4

SAVING INCENTIVES: WHAT MAY WORK, WHAT MAY NOT*

Thomas L. Hungerford

SUMMARY

Saving is the portion of national output that is not consumed and represents resources that can be used to increase, replace, or improve the nation's capital stock. The U.S. net national saving rate reached a post-war peak of 12.4% in 1965 and has then trended downward since to a low of -0.2% in 2008. Many analysts claim that saving is too low. Among the Organization for Economic Cooperation and Development (OECD) countries, the United States has the fourth lowest saving rate.

Survey evidence suggests that people know why they should save, but many don't save, especially lower-income individuals and families. Several reasons have been offered to explain the declining personal saving rate and the relatively high proportion of individuals and families that do not save. Economic reasons start from the premise that individuals and families are rational and make optimal decisions about consumption and saving throughout the life course. Low saving rates are then explained by economic disincentives induced by government policy or by life cycle changes in the propensity to save. Behavioral reasons start from the premise that individuals and families do not always make optimal decisions regarding consumption and saving.

---

* This is an edited, reformatted and augmented version of a Congressional Research Service publication, CRS Report for Congress RL33482, from www.crs.gov, dated March 5, 2010.

The government offers tax incentives to individuals and families to save. The empirical evidence on the relationship of tax incentives to the saving rate mostly comes from examinations of traditional individual retirement accounts (IRAs) and 401(k) plans. The reported results are mixed, but generally indicate small effects. Be that as it may, the tax incentives tend to benefit higher-income individuals and families to a much greater extent than lower-income individuals and families. The primary reasons are (1) higher-income individuals are much more likely to save, and (2) higher-income individuals face higher marginal tax rates and benefit more from sheltering income from taxation.

Furthermore, the tax revenue loss for these incentives lower public saving by reducing the budget surplus or increasing the budget deficit. For FY2009, these tax incentives are estimated to cost the U.S. Treasury $53.1 billion in forgone tax revenues. The Bush Administration and the 2005 President's Advisory Panel on Federal Tax Reform advocated expanding tax incentives as the primary policy to encourage personal saving. Research has shown that personal saving has been fairly unresponsive to tax incentives, however, and such incentives may substantially decrease public saving (that is, increase the budget deficit). The long-term net effect on national saving and economic growth is likely negative.

INTRODUCTION

From an individual's perspective, saving is "money in the bank." The increases in wealth that saving represents can be spent in the near future for emergencies or children's educational expenses, in the distant future for retirement, or passed down to heirs.[1] From a national perspective, however, saving is income that is not spent on consumption goods or services. That is, it is the portion of national output that is not consumed and represents resources that can be used to increase, replace, or improve the nation's capital stock.[2]

Many analysts claim that saving is too low. For example, recent research has shown that about a quarter of the U.S. population live in households whose assets are below 25% of the poverty threshold.[3] If housing wealth is not included, the proportion increases to over 40% of the U.S. population. Furthermore, retirement specialists argue that many people nearing retirement have not accumulated enough assets to maintain their present living standards after retirement.[4]

At the national level, analysts caution against a low savings rate. They argue that high capital investment is a good thing, but if it is not financed by national saving it has to be financed by borrowing abroad.[5] Persistent borrowing from abroad builds up international liabilities and implies increasing shares of national income will be sent overseas as interest and dividends. It is difficult to say that the U.S. national saving rate is too low since there is no universally accepted definition of what constitutes a low saving rate. But it is noteworthy that among the Organization for Economic Cooperation and Development (OECD) countries, the United States has the third lowest saving rate.[6]

The post-World War II trend in the U.S. saving rate (saving as a percentage of gross domestic product) is shown in Figure 1.[7] The net national saving rate (the heavy solid line) reached a postwar peak of 12.2% in 1965 and has trended downward since then reaching a low of -0.2% in 2008.

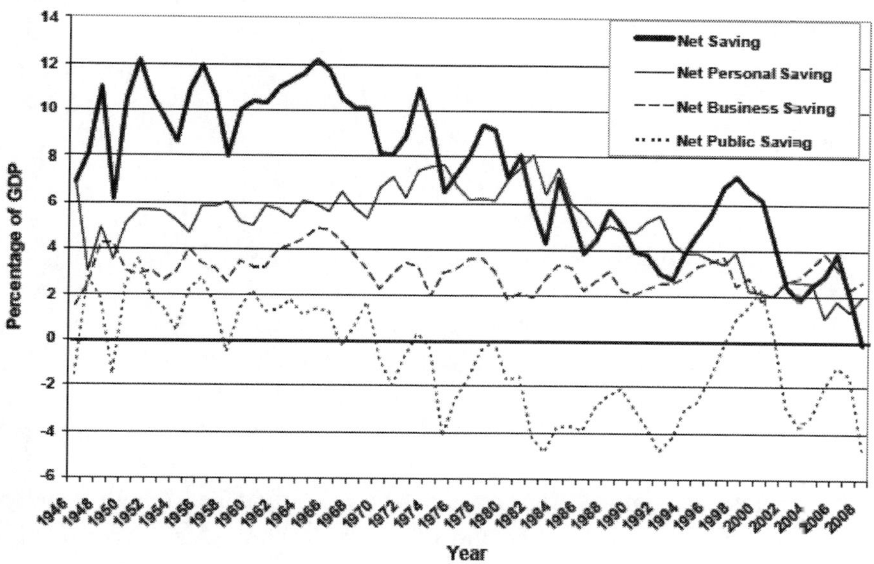

Source: Department of Commerce, Bureau of Economic Analysis.

Figure 1. Net National Saving Rates, 1946-2008.

There are three components to national saving. The first is personal saving or the saving by individuals and households (the light solid line in the figure). This is what people typically think of as saving. The second component is business saving, which consists of corporate retained earnings (the dashed line). The final component is public saving, which is federal, state, and local government surpluses (the dotted line). Public saving can be and often is negative if the government sector is running a deficit.

The decline in the national saving rate since 1965 has two main sources. First, the public saving rate fell from 1.4% in 1965 to -4.9% in 1983. Most of this decline in the public saving rate was due to increasing federal budget deficits. After 1982, the steady fall in the personal saving rate accounts for much of the decline in the national saving rate. The fall in the personal saving rate has been attributed to a combination of factors including the increase in transfer income (which is rarely saved), an increase in household wealth, and an increase in the proportion of the population 65 years or older (who tend to spend rather than accumulate savings).[8] Each of these could increase consumption relative to income, thus lowering saving.

In response to the perceived low saving rate, the government offers many saving incentives through the tax system. In addition, many employers offer some inducements to encourage their employees to save for retirement. This report examines why individuals and households save or don't save, and the effectiveness of the various incentives and inducements in increasing personal and national saving.

Reasons for Saving and Not Saving

John Maynard Keynes argued that there are eight primary reasons or motives leading individuals to save (that is, to forgo consumption):[9]

- Precaution motive: "To build up a reserve against unforeseen contingencies,"
- Foresight motive: "To provide for an anticipated future relation between the income and the needs of the individual or his family different from that which exists in the present,"
- Calculation motive: "To enjoy interest and appreciation,"
- Improvement motive: "To enjoy gradually increasing expenditures,"
- Independence motive: "To enjoy a sense of independence and the power to do things,"
- Enterprise motive: "To secure a *masse de manœuvre* to carry out speculative or business projects,"
- Pride (bequest) motive: "To bequeath a fortune," and
- Avarice motive: "To satisfy pure miserliness."

Others have added a down payment motive as a ninth reason for saving.[10] Recent survey evidence generally confirms that many of these motives are the main reasons why Americans save (see Table 1). The table reports the response of prime-aged heads of households grouped by age and income.[11]

Table 1. Reasons for Saving by Age and Income Group

	Ages 25-39		Ages 40-49		Ages 50-59	
	Bottom Half	Top Half	Bottom Half	Top Half	Bottom Half	Top Half
Retirement	15.2%	37.3%	23.6%	54.4%	37.2%	67.2%
Precautionary	30.1	33.4	36.3	22.2	29.6	20.1
House	11.4	3.7	4.8	1.3	3.1	0.8
Purchases	12.6	6.9	13.6	4.3	13.4	2.6
Education	16.2	11.5	9.4	14.3	4.6	6.2
Other	11.6	6.4	7.5	2.6	6.1	2.7
Can't Save	2.0	0.8	4.8	0.9	6.1	0.5

Source: CRS tabulation of 2007 Survey of Consumer Finances.
Note: Columns may not sum to 100% due to rounding.

Four major points can be made about these results. First, saving for retirement is generally the most important reason for saving in nearly every age and income group. The foresight or retirement motive is stronger for older age groups—the age groups closer to retirement. Furthermore, families in the upper half of the income distribution are more likely to cite saving for retirement as their primary reason for saving than those in the lower half of the income distribution.

Second, saving for the inevitable rainy day (the precaution motive) appears to be the primary reason for saving among younger families in the lower half of the income distribution. For the other groups, it is the second most frequently cited reason for saving. For the older two age groups, those with lower income are more likely to save for precautionary reasons than those with more income.

Third, within each age group, those in the lower half of the income distribution are more likely than those in the upper half to cite saving for future purchases of goods and services such as homes, home repairs, and durable goods as the most important reason to save. A possible explanation for this disparity by income is lower-income families may be credit constrained and have to save for purchases rather than using a credit card.

Lastly, among the youngest families, about one in seven report that education is the most important reason for saving (the improvement motive), but there is some difference between the two income groups. Older families, especially those in the oldest age group, are less likely to report this as an important reason for saving since their children are generally grown and finished with their formal education.

The results reported in Table 1 suggest that people know why they should save, but provides little information on whether or not they do save. Figure 2 shows the percentage of families in each age and income group who report not saving. There is relatively little variation across age groups—about 20% of the families do not save. There are large disparities, however, by income. About 10% of the families in the upper half of the income distribution report not saving. In contrast, about a third of the families in the lower half of the income distribution do not save.

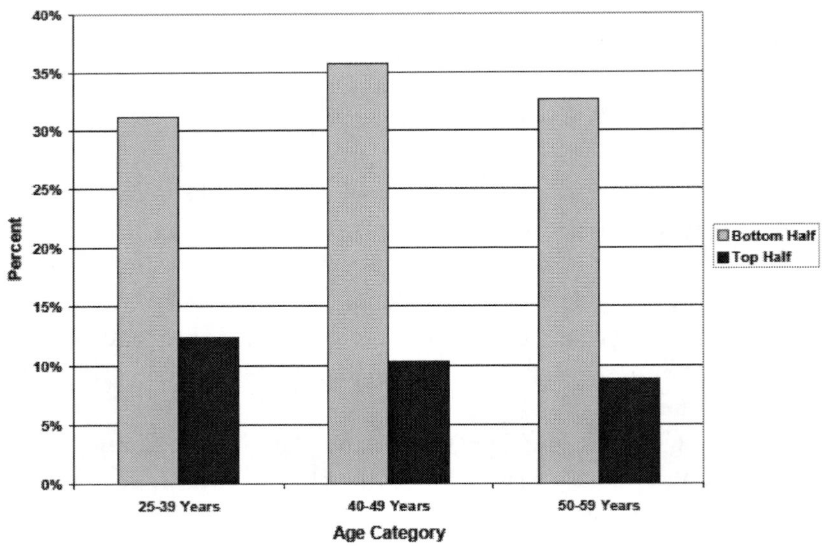

Source: CRS analysis of 2007 Survey of Consumer Finances.

Figure 2. Percentage of Households Not Saving By Age and Income Group.

Several reasons have been offered for the declining personal saving rate and the relatively high proportion of individuals and families that do not save. The economic reasons start from the premise that individuals and families are rational and make optimal decisions about consumption and saving throughout the life course. Low saving rates are then explained by economic disincentives induced by government policy or by life cycle changes in the propensity to save. Behavioral reasons start from the premise that individuals and families do not always make optimal decisions regarding consumption and saving.

Economic Reasons for Low Savings and Saving Rates

At the aggregate level, some analysts point out that the rising proportion of the elderly in the U.S. population may explain the declining saving rate. Since the elderly should dissave (that is, spend their savings) rather than save, the aggregate saving rate should fall. Research has shown, however, that saving rates do not vary that much across age groups, and the change in the age distribution in the 1980s was too small to explain the decline in the aggregate saving rate.[12]

Although the change in the age distribution of the U.S. population toward a higher proportion of elderly may not explain the fall in the saving rate, there is evidence that the elderly now are saving less than past cohorts of elderly. Research shows that there has been an increase in annuitization of wealth (especially Social Security and defined benefit pension wealth) which could be due to lessened bequest and precautionary motives.[13] Consequently, consumption by the elderly is higher and saving is lower. More elderly who are saving less may have had some effect on the personal saving rate. But this does not explain low saving rates for younger individuals.

Furthermore, this finding may change in the future with the shift from defined benefit pension plans to defined contribution pension plans (especially 401(k) plans), which do not have to be annuitized at retirement.

Some have argued that social welfare programs (social insurance and public assistance) have contributed to the decline in saving. Social insurance programs such as unemployment insurance and Social Security (both for disability and old age) may have reduced the need for precautionary saving.[14] But there have been no large scale changes in these programs since 1980 that could explain the trend in personal saving. Furthermore, recent research shows that the precautionary saving motive does not give rise to much wealth in the economy and probably to relatively little saving.[15]

A related argument suggests that asset-based, means-tested public assistance programs such as Temporary Assistance to Needy Families, Supplemental Security Income, and food stamps discourage saving by families with low expected lifetime earnings. Proponents of this argument point out that the asset test acts as an implicit 100% tax rate on savings "in the event of an earnings downturn or medical expense large enough to cause the household to seek welfare support."[16] This would prevent these families from saving for precautionary reasons and for retirement since most public assistance programs include both regular and retirement savings accounts as assets subject to the asset limit. This may help explain why lower-income families have little savings, but does not explain the decline in the personal saving rate since the mid-1980s because the means-testing rules of these programs have not substantially changed over the past 25 years. In addition, many low-income families do not save because after everyday living expenses are covered there is little or no money left over for saving.

Two financial explanations offered to explain declining saving rates are (1) capital gains in housing and equities, and (2) the development of financial markets. The increase in wealth from unrealized capital gains in housing and equities since 1990 allows individuals and families to maintain a target level of wealth (and even increase the target level) without active saving. The developments and expansion in credit cards and home equity loans mean families do not have to save as much for future durable good and home purchases.

Retirement saving has to last throughout the retirement years. Recent evidence suggests that individuals tend to underestimate how long they will live. Survey results show that a majority of Americans underestimate the life expectancy "for someone their own age and gender."[17] Similarly, British men and women underestimate how long they are likely to live by about five years.[18] Consequently, even if people are saving for retirement, they may be undersaving because they are saving for a shorter retirement period than what they will actually experience. This could help explain low levels of savings, but cannot explain the downward trend in personal saving rates unless there has been a change in Americans' underestimate of their life expectancy.

Behavioral Reasons for Low Savings and Saving Rates

In recent years, behavioral models have been developed to explain low savings and low saving rates, especially for retirement. The traditional economic model of saving, the life-cycle model, assumes that individuals make rational, far-sighted decisions. The theory implies that saving rates increase with age and savings accumulate until retirement when individuals begin to spend down their savings. The bulk of the empirical evidence, however, tends to not support the life-cycle model.[19] Unlike the traditional economic model for saving, behavioral models stress that individuals can and do make choices that are unfavorable to themselves. These models emphasize the role of inertia, the lack of self-control, and the limits of human intellectual capabilities.

Retirement savings accounts (for example, 401(k) plans and IRAs) require workers to be proactive and decide to participate, how much to save, and how to invest the retirement account assets. But through inertia, workers may never make or at least postpone making these critical decisions. Research shows that changing the "default" options in 401(k) plans so the workers have to decide *not* to participate can substantially increase participation rates in these plans and increase retirement saving.[20] Workers, through inertia, also tend to accept the default contribution rate and the investment allocation chosen by the plan administrator. Therefore, the defaults need to be carefully chosen to allow for an adequate return while protecting the worker's investment.

Saving takes will power. Individuals have to forgo current consumption in order to save for future consumption, and they may not have the self-control to forgo consumption.[21] Often individuals develop self-regulatory mechanisms or rules to control spending such as mental accounting systems. In a mental accounting system the individual treats money in different accounts as not being fungible, and has a different propensity to spend money from the different accounts. But equally as often individuals manipulate or bend their own rules of self-control.[22]

To make the complex decisions determining the optimal consumption path over a lifetime requires not only complete information on the economic environment, but also almost unlimited computing power. Individuals, however, rarely have complete information, and may not be able to adequately process the information they do have. To deal with human information processing limitations, individuals often use simple rules of thumb to make these complex decisions and generally accept alternatives that are "good enough" rather than optimal.[23] Consequently, individuals may make seemingly short-sighted decisions and save too little.

Many people nearing retirement age do not plan ahead and have not thought about retirement and financing their retirement. A recent study found that about a third of older Americans aged 50 to 61 years have not thought about retirement. Furthermore, those who have not thought about retirement have significantly lower net financial wealth than those who have thought about retirement (either a little or a lot).[24]

INDUCEMENTS TO SAVE

The government offers various incentives to individuals, families, and businesses to save. In addition, businesses offer a variety of inducements to encourage their employees to save for retirement. The incentives and inducements are designed to overcome one or more barriers to saving.

Tax Incentives

Tax incentives increase the effective rate of return on savings. Tax-favored savings plans for individuals and families are classified as either front-loaded or back-loaded.[25] In front-loaded plans, the contributions are tax deferred so the tax benefits primarily accrue at the time money is contributed to the account. The earnings grow tax-free until the funds are withdrawn or distributed. At that time, both the contributions and earnings are taxed. Traditional deductible IRAs and 401(k) plans are examples of a front-loaded savings accounts. In back-loaded plans, after-tax dollars are contributed to the account, and neither the contributions nor the earnings are taxed for qualified withdrawals. The Roth IRA is the best known example of a back-loaded savings account.

Both types of plans will yield a higher after-tax distribution than regular taxable savings accounts, thus providing an incentive to save in these accounts. As long as the tax rate is the same at the time of withdrawal as when the funds were contributed, both front-loaded and back-loaded savings accounts will yield the same after-tax distribution at retirement. Individuals who save for their children's education, on the one hand, often begin saving early in their working career when their earnings are relatively low, and tend to be in the lower tax brackets. They then withdraw the funds during their peak earning years when their children attend college. Consequently, they may be in a higher tax bracket when the monies are distributed from the savings account. A back-loaded plan may confer greater benefits than a front-loaded plan in this case. On the other hand, individuals saving for retirement often are in higher tax brackets during their working years than at retirement. For these individuals, a front-loaded plan may confer greater benefits. In either case, the saving decisions are often made several years before anticipated withdrawals, and it is difficult to know what tax bracket one will be in so far in advance.

These tax incentives, however, can affect both personal and public saving. The tax revenue loss for these incentives will lower public saving by reducing the budget surplus or increasing the budget deficit.[26] The reduction in public saving may more than offset any increase in personal saving induced by the tax incentives. The costs of front-and back-loaded savings plans are reflected in the federal budget at different times. For front-loaded plans, the tax expenditures are incurred immediately, and the revenues from taxing distributions occur in the future. But there are no immediate tax expenditures for back-loaded savings plans because only after-tax income is contributed to the account. The costs to the government are reflected in the budget only when the monies are distributed from the account. Over the long-term, a front-loaded plan may be less costly to the government than a back-loaded plan, but within the typical 5- or 10-year budget window, the back-loaded plan will look less expensive.

The tax expenditures of these tax incentives are not trivial. Table 2 reports the estimated tax expenditures for the exclusion of contributions and earnings for employer pension plans such as 401(k) plans, IRAs, and Keogh plans, in addition to the Saver's Credit which is discussed below. The Joint Committee on Taxation estimates that the FY2009 retirement income related tax expenditures will amount to $53.1 billion. By FY2013, these tax expenditures are estimated to reach $169.0 billion, which is equivalent to almost one-third of the projected budget deficit for that year.

Table 2. Estimates of Tax Expenditures, 2009-2013(billions of dollars)

			Fiscal Year		
	2009	**2010**	**2011**	**2012**	**2013**
Employer Plans	$71.0	$67.1	$84.1	$106.1	$131.7
IRAs	-27.9	25.1	17.5	19.2	24.1
Keogh Plans	9.2	12.9	16.2	17.3	17.8
Saver's Credit	0.9	0.9	0.9	1.0	1.0
Total	**53.1**	**102.4**	**114.6**	**138.7**	**169.0**

Source: U.S. Congress, Joint Committee on Taxation, *Estimates of Federal Tax Expenditures For Fiscal Years 2009- 2013*, committee print, 111th Congress, 2nd sess., Jan. 11, 2010 (Washington: GPO 2010).

Furthermore, conventional economic theory and empirical analysis do not offer unambiguous evidence that these tax incentives have increased personal saving. From a theoretical perspective, the effect of a tax reduction on personal saving is ambiguous because of offsetting income and substitution effects. The increased rate of return may cause individuals to substitute future consumption for current consumption and save more (a substitution effect), but, at the same time, the higher rate of return allows individuals to save less and still obtain their target amount of savings (an income effect). The overall consequences for personal savings depends on the relative magnitude of these two effects. In the case of IRAs, personal savings may be unaffected because most of the tax benefits are provided to individuals contributing the maximum amount, which eliminates any substitution effect. Casual observation suggests that the income effect dominates since the personal saving rate has fallen since the introduction of IRAs and 401(k) plans. The empirical evidence on the relationship of tax incentives to the saving rate mostly comes from examinations of traditional IRAs and 401(k) plans. The reported results are mixed, but generally indicate small effects.[27] Furthermore, Roth IRAs eliminate the immediate reward to retirement saving because the contributions are not tax deductible and may thus reduce saving.

In general, many tax incentives to increase saving tend to benefit higher-income individuals and families to a much greater extent than lower-income individuals and families. The primary reasons are (1) higher-income individuals are much more likely to save, and (2) higher-income individuals face higher marginal tax rates and benefit more from sheltering income from taxation. Furthermore, with regards to educational savings plans, the penalties for using the educational savings for non-educational purposes may discourage lower-income families from having these accounts. Children from lower-income families are less likely to attend college than other children, thus increasing the likelihood of being penalized for having an education savings account. These penalties partly explain why parents participating in Coverdell Education Savings Accounts (ESAs) and 529 plans have substantially higher income, on average, than other parents.[28]

The Economic Growth and Tax Relief Reconciliation Act of 2001 (P.L. 107-16) provided low-and moderate-income individuals a nonrefundable tax credit for contributions to a qualified retirement plan (the Saver's Credit).[29] The maximum amount of the tax credit is $2,000. The savings effects of this tax credit have not been fully evaluated yet, but early evidence suggests that many taxpayers are unable to receive the full benefit because the credit is nonrefundable.[30] In addition, the Saver's Credit appears to be substantially less effective in boosting saving among low-income individuals than a simple matching contribution possibly because of the complexity of the Saver's Credit and the tax system in general.[31]

Other Inducements

There are at least four other inducements that have been used to encourage savings for specific purposes. First, an initial or supplemental contribution can be placed in an individual's savings account. An example is the 1% agency contribution placed in a federal employee's Thrift Savings Plan (TSP) account.[32] This contribution is placed in the account whether or not the employee chooses to make contributions to his or her account. This can encourage individuals to save by overcoming the inertia to open an account, and it allows individuals to observe the benefits of saving (for example, interest compounding) without risking their own money. Once the benefits of saving are experienced, individuals may be more willing to commit their own funds to the savings account.

Second, matching contributions can be made to an individual's account. This is a common practice in many 401(k) pension plans, including the federal Thrift Saving Plan. In the case of 401(k) pensions, part or all of an employee's contribution is matched by the employer. The more the employee contributes, the more the employer contributes up to a limit. The employer is essentially supplementing the employee's salary, but only if the employee saves. Empirical evidence suggests that small matching contributions (about 10 cents for every dollar saved) will increase employees' contributions. But increasing matching contributions past this point may have no effect on an employee's contributions or actually reduce his or her contributions.[33] If an employee has a set target for saving, for example, then increasing the employer's contribution means that the employee can save less and still meet his or her saving target. Limited evidence suggests that matching contributions could significantly increase contributions by low-and moderate-income families.[34]

Third, tax-favored savings initially could be used only for a specific purpose, such as retirement in the case of 401(k) plans, and individuals faced a penalty for nonqualified uses of the savings. The penalty helps commit individuals to hold the funds for the desired purpose (such as retirement) rather than use them for current consumption. But individuals may be reluctant to give up the freedom to use the funds for other equally important purposes as individuals try to balance saving for retirement and saving for precautionary reasons. Over time, however, laws and regulations were changed to allow employees to borrow from their 401(k) plan or to make penalty-free withdrawals for emergency purposes. In addition to retirement after age 591/2, qualified (that is, penalty-free) distributions can be made from IRAs for educational expenses, first-time home purchase, and medical expenses. There is some empirical evidence that pre-retirement access to 401(k) funds increases participation in and contributions to 401(k) pension plans.[35] But allowing pre-retirement access to 401(k) assets could also lead some to have smaller pension balances at retirement if the borrowed funds are never repaid or if withdrawn funds are never replaced.

Fourth, some firms have experimented with changing the default options for pension plans where participation is voluntary. For example, employees are covered by a firm's 401(k) plan only if they actively sign up and enroll in the plan. However, through inertia many employees do not participate. The default option, therefore, combines with worker inertia to yield low saving rates and little retirement savings. Changing the default to automatic enrollment means the employee has to actively opt out of the pension plan.[36] Recent evaluations of some firms that have changed to automatic enrollment shows that participation is significantly increased though this simple change. But through inertia, a substantial fraction of the new participants accept the firm's default contribution level and investment options for their pension assets.[37]

PROPOSALS TO INCREASE SAVING

The 2005 President's Advisory Panel on Federal Tax Reform proposed the creation of Save for Family Accounts (SFAs) to replace existing education and medical savings accounts, and Save for Retirement Accounts (SRAs) to replace traditional and Roth IRAs. This proposal would have allowed every taxpayer to contribute up to $10,000 every year to an SFA and an SRA on an after-tax basis.[38] The earnings would have accumulated tax-free in the same way as in the current Roth IRA. Tax-free withdrawals would have been allowed at any time from the SFA for qualified educational and medical costs, or to purchase a primary residence. In addition, taxpayers would have been able to withdraw up to $1,000 tax-free each year for any purpose. Nonqualified distributions in excess of the $1,000 limit would have been subject to income taxes and a 10% penalty tax, similar to the penalty paid on nonqualified distributions from the current Roth IRA. Tax-free withdrawals from SRAs would have been allowed after age 58, death, or disability. Nonqualified withdrawals would have been subject to the income tax and a 10% penalty tax.

The President's Advisory Panel plan would shift savings incentives from the front-loaded form to the back-loaded form. Most of the arguments regarding increasing private saving, however, apply to front-loaded savings plans. Back-loaded plans or Roth IRAs eliminate (1) the immediate reward to retirement saving (the tax deduction), and (2) the need to save for future tax liabilities. Consequently, shifting from front-loaded to back-loaded savings approaches may reduce personal savings. In addition, the long-term revenue loss from these proposals could be substantial thus leading to a large reduction in public saving.[39] The result of these savings proposals could be a large reduction in national saving and a reduction in economic growth.

A proposal offered by analysts at the Brookings Institution moves away from reliance on tax incentives to encourage retirement saving.[40] The proposal has several elements designed to remove behavioral barriers to saving. The two major elements are (1) automatic enrollment in 401(k) plans or in an IRA if the employer does not sponsor a pension plan, and (2) a 30% government matching contribution. The government contribution would replace the current tax deduction for retirement saving contributions. Other elements include allowing participants to borrow from their retirement account, and removing retirement savings from the asset test for public assistance eligibility.

The Obama Administration's savings proposals also are designed to remove behavioral barriers to saving. First, the Administration proposed to require employers that do not offer a retirement plan to offer employers automatic enrollment in an IRA.[41] Second, the maximum temporary business tax credit to small employers (100 or fewer employees) adopting a new qualified retirement plan would be doubled (from $500 to $1,000) per year for three years. Third, the Administration proposed to expand the Saver's Credit by making it refundable and converting it to a 50% match on up to $500 in retirement saving.

CONCLUSIONS

Various motives have been identified as to why people save, and survey evidence suggests that people know why they should save. However, many people do not save. Many reasons have been offered to explain low saving rates and low savings. Economic barriers to saving include disincentives induced by government policies and life-cycle changes in the propensity to save. Behavioral explanations for low savings stress that individuals can make choices that are unfavorable to themselves. To overcome these barriers, the government offers a variety of saving incentives.

Most of the government incentives to save come through the tax system. For FY2009, these tax incentives are estimated to cost the U.S. Treasury $53.1

billion in forgone tax revenues and are projected to grow to $169.0 billion by FY2013—equivalent to about a third of the projected FY2013 budget deficit. The tax incentives primarily benefit higher-income families because they (1) are more likely to save, and (2) face higher marginal tax rates and thus benefit more from sheltering income from taxation. The tax incentives, however, appear to be relatively ineffective in inducing new saving—many of the families benefitting from the tax incentives likely shifted funds from other saving accounts into the tax-preferred accounts. Consequently, public saving is lower because of the forgone tax revenues due to the tax incentives while personal saving may be only slightly increased at best. In designing pro-saving policies, it is important to consider the aggregate effects of the policies on all components of national savings, both public and private.

The 2005 President's Advisory Panel on Federal Tax Reform advocated expanding tax incentives as the primary policy to encourage saving. Personal saving has been shown to be fairly unresponsive to tax incentives, however, and they may substantially decrease public saving (that is, increase the budget deficit). The long-term net effect on national saving is likely negative. The Obama Administration's savings proposals appear to be designed to (1) overcome behavioral barriers to saving, and (2) redistribute the benefits of government saving incentives more broadly across the population. These proposals could increase personal saving, but could also decrease public saving.

End Notes

[1] The term saving refers to the flow of resources not consumed and represents additions to wealth. Savings is a synonym for wealth.

[2] See CRS Report RL30873, *Saving in the United States: How Has It Changed and Why Is It Important?*, by Brian W. Cashell and Gail E. Makinen.

[3] See Asena Caner and Edward N. Wolff, "Asset Poverty in the United States, 1984-1999: Evidence from the Panel Study of Income Dynamics," *Review of Income and Wealth*, vol. 50, no. 4 (Dec. 2004), pp. 493-518. The authors adopt the definition of "asset poor" as a household whose "access to 'wealth-type resources' is insufficient to enable the household to meet its 'basic needs' for some limited 'period of time.'" They choose the poverty threshold as their definition of basic needs and three months as the limited period of time.

[4] See, for example, B. Douglas Bernheim and John Karl Scholz, "Private Saving and Public Policy," in James M. Poterba, ed., *Tax Policy and the Economy, Vol. 7* (Cambridge, MA: MIT Press, 1993), pp. 73-110; and Alicia H. Munnell, Anthony Webb, and Luke Delorme, *A New National Retirement Risk Index*, Center for Retirement Research at Boston College, Issue Brief no. 48, Jun. 2006.

[5] See, for example, Edward Gramlich, "The Importance of Raising National Saving," speech at the Benjamin Rush Lecture, Dickinson College, PA, Mar. 2, 2005.

[6] Only Iceland and Portugal have lower national saving rates than the United States. See *OECD in Figures*, OECD Observer 2006, Supplement 1.

[7] The figure shows net saving rather than gross saving. Gross saving includes depreciation allowances destined to replace existing capital. Net saving represents resources from forgoing consumption that are available to increase the stock of capital.

[8] See David W. Wilcox, "Household Spending and Saving: Measurement, Trends, and Analysis," *Federal Reserve Bulletin*, vol. 77, no. 1 (Jan. 1991), pp. 1-17.

[9] John Maynard Keynes, *The General Theory of Employment, Interest and Money* (London: MacMillan and Co., 1936), pp. 107-108.

[10] See Martin Browning and Annamaria Lusardi, "Household Saving: Micro Theories and Micro Facts," *Journal of Economic Literature*, vol. 34, no. 4 (Dec. 1996), pp. 1797-1855. As an example, qualifying for a mortgage with no private mortgage insurance requires a down payment of 20%.

[11] Families are divided into the top half or the bottom half of the income distribution based on total family income.

[12] See Alan J. Auerbach and Laurence J. Kotlikoff, "Demographics, Fiscal Policy, and U.S. Saving in the 1980s and Beyond," in Lawrence H. Summers, ed., *Tax Policy and the Economy, Vol. 4* (Cambridge, MA: MIT Press, 1990), pp. 73-101.

[13] See Alan J. Auerbach, Laurence J. Kotlikoff, and David N. Weil, *The Increasing Annuitization of the Elderly—Estimates and Implications for Intergenerational Transfers, Inequality, and National Saving*, National Bureau of Economic Research, Working Paper no. 4182, Oct. 1992.

[14] See Lawrence Summers and Chris Carrol, "Why Is U.S. National Saving So Low?" Brookings Institution, *Brookings Papers on Economic Activity*, no. 1, 1987, pp. 607-635.

[15] See Erik Hurst, Annamaria Lusardi, Arthur Kennickell, and Francisco Torralba, *Precautionary Savings and the Importance of Business Owners*, National Bureau of Economic Research, Working Paper no. 11731, Nov. 2005.

[16] R. Glenn Hubbard, Jonathan Skinner, and Stephen P. Zeldes, "Precautionary Saving and Social Insurance," *Journal of Political Economy*, vol. 103, no. 2 (1995), p. 393.

[17] Society of Actuaries, *2005 Risks and Process of Retirement Survey: Report of Findings*, Mar. 2006, p. 5.

[18] Chris O'Brien, Paul Fenn, and Stephen Diacon, *How Long Do People Expect to Live? Results and Implications*, Centre for Risk and Insurance Studies, Research Report 2005-1, June 2005.

[19] See, for example, Paul Courant, Edward Gramlich, and John Laitner, "A Dynamic Micro Estimate of the Life Cycle Model," in Henry J. Aaron and Gary Burtless, eds., *Retirement and Economic Behavior* (Washington, DC: Brookings Institution, 1986); and B. Douglas Bernheim, Jonathan Skinner, and Steven Weinberg, "What Accounts for the Variation in Retirement Wealth Among U.S. Households?" *American Economic Review*, vol. 91, no. 4 (Sept. 2001), pp. 832-857.

[20] Brigitte C. Madrian and Dennis F. Shea, "The Power of Suggestion: Inertia in 401(k) Participation and Savings Behavior," *Quarterly Journal of Economics*, vol. 116, no. 4 (Nov. 2001), pp. 1149-1187.

[21] See, for example, Richard H. Thaler, "Psychology and Savings Policies," *American Economic Review*, vol. 84, no. 2 (May 1994), pp. 186-192.

[22] Amar Cheema and Dilip Soman, "Malleable Mental Accounting: The Effect of Flexibility on the Justification of Attractive Spending and Consumption Decisions," *Journal of Consumer Psychology*, vol. 16, no. 1 (2006), pp. 33-44.

[23] See, for example, Herbert A. Simon, *The Sciences of the Artificial, 2nd Edition* (Cambridge, MA: MIT Press, 1981).

[24] Annamaria Lusardi, "Information, Expectations, and Savings for Retirement," in Henry J. Aaron, ed., *Behavioral Dimensions of Retirement Economics* (Washington, DC: Brookings Institution, 1999).

[25] For a discussion of many of the issues with regards to IRAs see CRS Report RL30255, *Individual Retirement Accounts (IRAs): Issues and Proposed Expansion*, coordinated by Thomas L. Hungerford and Jane G. Gravelle.

[26] The cost of tax incentives are measured in terms of tax expenditures, which are estimates of the revenue losses attributable to provisions of federal tax laws.

[27] For a more complete discussion of the savings literature, see Jane G. Gravelle, *The Economic Effects of Taxing Capital Income* (Cambridge, MA: MIT Press, 1994), p. 27 for a discussion of the general empirical literature on savings and pp. 193-197 for a discussion of the empirical studies of IRAs. Subsequent to this survey, a paper by Orazio P. Attanasio and Thomas C. DeLeire, "The Effect of Individual Retirement Accounts on Household Consumption and National Savings," *Economic Journal*, vol. 112 (July 2002), pp. 504-538 found little evidence that IRAs increased savings. For additional surveys see the three articles published in the *Journal of Economic Perspectives*, vol. 10, no. 3 (Fall 1996): R. Glenn Hubbard and Jonathan Skinner, "Assessing the Effectiveness of Savings Incentives," (pp. 73-90); James M. Poterba, Steven F. Venti and David A. Wise, "How Retirement Savings Programs Increase Saving," (pp. 91- 113); Eric M. Engen, William G. Gale, and John Karl Scholz, "The Illusory Effects of Savings Incentives on Saving," (pp. 113-138). A working paper by Alun Thomas and Christopher Towe, "U.S. Private Saving and the Tax Treatment of IRA/401(k)s: A Re-examination Using Household Saving Data," International Monetary Fund working paper 96/87 Aug. 1996 found that IRAs did not increase private household saving. A more recent study by Eric M. Engen and William G. Gale found that 401(k) plans, which are similar to IRAs in important ways, had a negligible to modest effect on savings. See "The Effects of 401(k) Plans on Household Wealth: Differences Across Earnings Groups," National Bureau for Economic Research working paper 8032, Dec. 2000. See also Douglas H. Joines and James G. Manegold, "IRAs and Savings: Evidence from a Panel of Taxpayers," Federal Reserve Bank of Kansas City research working paper 91-05, Oct. 1991; Daniel J. Benjamin, "Does 401(k) Eligibility Increase Saving? Evidence from Propensity Score Subclassification," Journal of Public Economics, vol. 83, no. 5-6 (2003), pp. 1259-1290; and Orazio P. Attanasio, James Banks, and Matthew Wakefield, "Effectiveness of Tax Incentives to Boost (Retirement) Savings: Theoretical Motivation and Empirical Evidence," *OECD Economic Studies* No. 39, 2004/2, pp. 145-172, which all present evidence that retirement saving tax incentives induce very little new saving.

[28] See Susan Dynarski, "Who Benefits from the Education Saving Incentives? Income, Educational Expectations and the Value of the 529 and Coverdell," *National Tax Journal*, vol. 57, no. 2 (June 2004), pp. 359-383; Sarah Holden, "Saving for College with 529 Plans," paper presented the Ninety-fifth Annual Conference on Taxation, Orlando, FL, Nov. 16, 2002; and Jennifer Ma, *Education Saving Incentives and Household Saving: Evidence from the 2000 TIAA-CREF Survey of Participants*, National Bureau of Economic Research Working Paper no. 9505, Feb. 2003.

[29] For a description of the Saver's Credit see William G. Gale, J. Mark Iwry, and Peter Orszag, *The Saver's Credit: Expanding Retirement Savings for Middle-and Lower-Income Americans*, The Retirement Security Project, Issue Brief no. 2005-2, Mar. 2005.

[30] See Gary Koenig and Robert Harvey, "Utilization of the Saver's Credit: An Analysis of the First Year," *National Tax Journal*, vol. 58, no. 4 (Dec. 2005), pp. 787-806.

[31] See Ester Duflo, William Gale, Jeffrey Liebman, Peter Orszag, and Emmanuel Saez, *Saving Incentives for Low-and Middle-Income Families: Evidence from a Field Experiment with H&R Block*, National Bureau of Economic Research, Working Paper no. 11680, Sept. 2005.

[32] This applies only to federal employees in the Federal Employee Retirement System (FERS) system and not to employees in the Civil Service Retirement System (CSRS).

[33] See Leslie E. Papke, "Participation in and Contributions to 401(k) Pension Plans: Evidence from Plan Data," *Journal of Human Resources*, vol. 30, no. 2 (Spring 1995), pp. 311-325.

[34] See Ester Duflo, William Gale, Jeffrey Liebman, Peter Orszag, and Emmanuel Saez, *Saving Incentives for Low-and Middle-Income Families: Evidence from a Field Experiment with H&R Block*, National Bureau of Economic Research, Working Paper no. 11680, Sept. 2005.

[35] U.S. Government Accountability Office, *401(k) Pension Plans: Loan Provisions Enhance Participation But May Affect Income Security for Some*, GAO/HEHS-98-5, Oct. 1997.

[36] For a review of IRS rulings regarding automatic enrollment in 401(k) plans, see CRS Report RS21954, *Automatic Enrollment in 401(k) Plans*, by Patrick Purcell.

[37] See Brigitte C. Madrian and Dennis F. Shea, "The Power of Suggestion: Inertia in 401(k) Participation and Savings Behavior," *Quarterly Journal of Economics*, vol. 116, no. 4 (Nov. 2001), pp. 1149-1187.

[38] Contributions to the SRA could not have exceeded earnings.

[39] See CRS Report RL32228, *Proposed Savings Accounts: Economic and Budgetary Effects*, by Jane G. Gravelle and Maxim Shvedov. The report suggests that the 10-year cost after 2015 of the Administration's proposal could have been in the neighborhood of $300 to $500 billion.

[40] See William G. Gale, Jonathan Gruber, and Peter R. Orszag, *Improving Opportunities and Incentives for Saving by Middle-and Low-Income Households*, Brookings Institution, Hamilton Project White Paper no. 2006-02, Apr. 2006.

[41] Employers with less than 10 employees or in existence for less than two years would be exempt.

INDEX

D

E

F

G

H

I

J

K

L

S

T

U

V

W

Y